Prodigal People

Books by Woodrow Kroll

Bible Country
Early in the Morning
Prodigal People
The Vanishing Ministry

Books by Don Hawkins

When Cancer Comes
Worry-Free Living
How to Beat Burnout
Before Burnout
Never Give Up
Prodigal People

Prodigal People

Coming Home to Right Relationships

Woodrow Kroll & Don Hawkins

kregel
PUBLICATIONS

Grand Rapids, MI 49501

Prodigal People: Coming Home to Right Relationships
by Woodrow Kroll and Don Hawkins.

Copyright © 1995 by Back to the Bible.

Published by Kregel Publications, a division of Kregel, Inc.,
P.O. Box 2607, Grand Rapids, MI 49501. Kregel Publications
provides trusted, biblical publications for Christian growth and
service. Your comments and suggestions are valued.

Cover Photograph: UNIPHOTO
Cover & Book Design: Alan G. Hartman

Library of Congress Cataloging-in-Publication Data
Kroll, Woodrow Michael, 1944–
   Prodigal people: coming home to right relationships /
Woodrow Kroll, Don Hawkins.
     p. cm.
   1. Prodigal son (Parable). 2. Christian life. I. Hawkins,
Don. II. Title.
BT378.P8K76   1995   226.8'06—dc20   94-48392
                                               CIP

ISBN 0-8254-3050-x (paperback)

1 2 3 4 5 Printing / Year 99 98 97 96 95

Printed in the United States of America

Contents

Part One: *The Parable of the Prodigal Son*

Part Two: *Portraits of Prodigals*

5

Part Three: *Modern Prodigals and Those Who Love Them*

Acknowledgments

We would like to express our appreciation to our wives, Linda Kroll and Kathy Hawkins, for their encouragement and to our colleagues at Back to the Bible for their support.

Special thanks to: Beth Nielson who spent many hours organizing material; Ruth Anne Franks who likewise invested many hours typing and retyping the manuscript; and Dawn Leuschen and Melissa Donegan who assisted with early portions of the text.

Thanks also to: Cathy Strate for handling many administrative tasks that allowed us to complete this project; Neil Craig and Sandy Schindler for help with some of the research; and Allen Bean for reviewing the final manuscript and offering many helpful suggestions.

Finally, special thanks to Dennis Hillman who was the point person for the Kregel publishing team. Without his tireless work of editing and polishing the various versions of the manuscript, this project could not have been completed.

Most of all, we thank the Lord God for providing the kind of love for prodigals without which there could be no book of this kind.

Preface

Then He said, "A certain man had two sons. And the younger of them said to his father, 'Father, give me the portion of goods that falls to me.' So he divided to them his livelihood. And not many days after, the younger son gathered all together, journeyed to a far country, and there wasted his possessions with prodigal living. But when he had spent all, there arose a severe famine in that land, and he began to be in want. Then he went and joined himself to a citizen of that country, and he sent him into his fields to feed swine. And he would gladly have filled his stomach with the pods that the swine ate, and no one gave him anything. But when he came to himself, he said, 'How many of my father's hired servants have bread enough and to spare, and I perish with hunger! I will arise and go to my father, and will say to him, "Father, I have sinned against heaven and before you, and I am no longer worthy to be called your son. Make me like one of your hired servants."' And he arose and came to his father. But when he was still a great way off, his father saw him and had compassion, and ran and fell on his neck and kissed him. And the son said to him, 'Father, I have sinned against heaven and in your sight, and am no longer worthy to be called your son.' But the father said to his servants, 'Bring out the best robe and put it on him, and put a ring on his hand and sandals on his feet. And bring the fatted calf here and kill it, and let us eat and be merry; for this my son was dead and is alive again; he was lost and is found.' And they began to be merry. Now his older son was in the field. And as he came and drew near to the house, he heard music and *dancing. So he called one of the servants and asked what these things meant. And he said to him, 'Your brother has come, and because he has received him safe and sound, your father has killed the fatted calf.' But he was angry and would not go in. Therefore his father came out and pleaded with him. So he answered and said to his father, 'Lo, these many years I have been serving you; I never transgressed your commandment at any time; and yet you never gave me a young goat, that I might make merry with my friends. But as soon as this son of yours came, who has devoured your livelihood with harlots, you killed the fatted calf for him.' And he said to him, 'Son, you are always with me, and all that I have is yours. It was right that we should make merry and be glad, for your brother was dead and is alive again, and was lost and is found.' " (Luke 15:11–32)*

Prodigal—It's not something you would appreciate being called nor would you make friends with someone by using it to refer to them. The word is loaded with emotion, especially for those who have been exposed to the teachings of the Bible. Both of us were raised by fathers who loved and respected God's Word and who communicated it to their children. We both can vividly recall being cautioned against prodigal behavior by parents who cared enough to issue such a warning.

So we have written this book, first of all, for "prodigals"—those who for one reason or another have strayed from the standard of behavior set forth in the Bible. We especially want to reach those who are living away from a loving heavenly Father—men and women who have never entered a right relationship with God through faith in the life-changing work of Jesus Christ, His Son.

We've also addressed individuals who may not have taken the prodigal's path but who really aren't sure where they stand, who feel an uneasiness that may represent God's personal conviction at work in their lives.

Finally, this book is for bystanders, watching the glad reunion take place, yet refusing to participate in the celebration. Some of us may be surprised to discover that we are actually "elder brothers," playing a prominent yet tragic role in this familiar story.

An Artistic Masterpiece

All the characters about whom we've written in this book are depicted in an incredible masterpiece entitled "The Return of the Prodigal" and painted in the eighteenth century by the Dutch master, Rembrandt. This larger-than-life painting was secured by Catherine the Great of

Russia in 1776 and placed in the Hermitage in St. Petersburg where it still hangs. The painting has been frequently copied, and it is said that on many occasions the line of people waiting to get into the Hermitage museum to see this magnificent work stretches for a mile or more.

It is a painting of majestic beauty, marked by a warm array of reds, yellows, and browns. It contains five characters: a young man dressed in a ragged yellow tunic, kneeling before an aged father clothed in a red cloak who reaches out to embrace his son. Standing nearby is a younger replica of the father also dressed in a red cloak. Using artistic license, Rembrandt includes two additional bystanders—one standing, the other sitting, both clearly in the background.

Jesus' story not only motivated Rembrandt's mural, it has also prompted some of the world's greatest preachers to craft sermons on this familiar parable. Our colleague, Warren Wiersbe, has put together an anthology of ten of these sermon masterpieces representing centuries of reflection on the deep significance of this story.[1]

Our purpose is not to duplicate the work of those preachers nor of numerous other Bible teachers who have addressed this story. Rather, we want to use the story of prodigal behavior as recorded in Luke 15 as a "benchmark." Jesus told the story to a group of bystanders who were unhappy with His socializing with tax collectors and sinners. In part one we study His response, in the form of this parable, which established a true standard for evaluating all prodigals—their situations and their potential—for all time.

In part two we broaden our focus to include portraits of other prodigals from the Bible. Our list is not exhaustive, but it does include numerous individuals—men and women—who wandered from God, often intentionally, who blundered tragically, and who frequently saw their lives fall apart in spectacular fashion. Encouragingly, many of them found their way back home, picked up the pieces, and started over.

We conclude our consideration of prodigalism in part three with a loving challenge to those who are prodigals, a word of encouragement and hope to those who love them, and a clear-cut appeal to older brothers for a change of heart regarding those who have taken the prodigal way.

In some cases names have been altered in order to insure the privacy of those who have allowed us to share their stories. Several cases cited are composites of various persons and circumstances we've encountered.

Our overall objective is to focus attention where Jesus directed it, not primarily toward either of the brothers and certainly not on any of the bystanders but rather toward the compassionate father.

He is the one who clearly parallels the heavenly Father eagerly looking for each prodigal's return and intently prepared to show His grace, love, and forgiveness in a way that totally transcends human understanding.

Endnotes

1. *Classic Sermons on the Prodigal Son* by Warren Wiersbe (Grand Rapids: Kregel Publications, 1990) includes sermons by notable preachers from the past such as Dwight L. Moody, Charles H. Spurgeon, and Martyn Lloyd-Jones.

Introduction

Jerry sat on a couch in his pastor's office, wringing his hands, his face taut with frustration.

"I just don't know what to do about Marcy, Pastor. I warned her last week that if she kept on writing checks we didn't have money in the bank for, they'd arrest her. Now, sure enough, they have. Her parents are totally flabbergasted. They just can't believe it. I just feel humiliated. Of course, she does too."

Some people would laughingly label Marcy's behavior as check bouncing or writing hot checks. The law, however, views it as a criminal offense. Jerry's pastor compassionately pointed out that this young wife and mother of a two-year-old had clearly engaged in what can be referred to as prodigal behavior.

Other Prodigals

This was not the young pastor's first exposure to prodigal behavior. During that same month he had counseled the parents of Phyllis, a teenage girl who had come home one evening to announce to her parents, "I'm pregnant and I'm thinking about having an abortion." He had also invested time talking with Rita, a distraught wife, Sunday school teacher, and mother of three, whose chance encounter with her husband, Calvin, and a female colleague from his office in the coffee shop of a hotel led to an angry confrontation in which Calvin admitted he was having an affair that he had no intention of giving up. And in response to an urgent phone call, the pastor had stopped by to visit the parents of eighteen-year-old Dean who had just been suspended from school because of poor grades, a refusal to attend classes, and persistent alcohol and drug abuse.

Just exactly what is a prodigal, anyway?

The dictionary defines a prodigal as one who is "exceedingly or recklessly wasteful, a spendthrift," "someone who spends or gives lavishly or foolishly." Ironically, the Latin roots of the word come from two words, the prefix *pro* which means "for," and the verb *agere* which means "to drive."[1]

In our culture these word roots seem to hint at an additional shade of meaning since we often use the word "prodigal" to refer to someone who is driven to foolishly abandon something of great value, which is exactly what the prodigal son described in Luke's gospel did. This young man chose something of lesser worth—a profligate lifestyle which he ultimately discovered to be of no real value whatsoever. Ultimately this young prodigal admitted the harmful effects of his prodigal behavior. So we'll describe a prodigal as one who foolishly abandons that which has greater value for something of lesser or no value. That's exactly the experience of Marcy, Phyllis, Calvin, and Dean.

Two Kinds of Prodigals

While throughout this book we'll examine prodigals who spent material goods lavishly and wastefully, we will also focus on prodigals whose behavior is directed against God, the loving Father. As we understand the human condition, there are two kinds of prodigals. We might label them prodigal unbelievers and prodigal believers. The prodigal unbeliever has never come to a relationship with God through faith. Because of the sin that separates this individual from God, we would consider him or her to be what the Bible refers to as spiritually "lost."

The second kind of prodigal is the believer, one who has had an authentic experience of faith in God but has chosen a path of disobedience, turned his or her back on the God who loves each one, and engaged in deliberate and self-destructive sinfulness.

Some biblical interpreters say the story of the lost son is primarily one of restoration of the spiritual relationship of those who are already members of God's spiritual family. Certainly, it has valuable application to such a situation. However, Christ delivered this story in pointed fashion to a collection of people, including a number of the highly-religious Pharisees who had rejected God's way of salvation and substituted their own works of human goodness. Furthermore, the restored prodigal was given a new, more significant relationship with his father than what he had enjoyed before (Luke 15:22).

Identifying Prodigal Behavior

Since a prodigal is one who rejects that which has greater value for that which has less—one who frequently spends lavishly and foolishly—the spiritual prodigal squanders God's gifts and blessings just as the prodigal son of Jesus' parable wasted his own inheritance.

Sometimes, like Marcy, prodigals wind up squandering money they don't have, with devastating financial and even legal consequences. Often, like Calvin, they squander cherished relationships, or like Phyllis, they give up that which can never be recaptured. Like Dean, they may sacrifice personal health and long-term well-being on the altar of immediate, undisciplined gratification.

Prodigals may waste physical strength or mental prowess, personal relationships or potential long-term relationships, mental and physical abilities or spiritual gifts. Money and time are frequently frittered away in the pursuit of useless or sinful pleasures while disciplines, virtues, and things that matter go neglected.

The results of prodigal behavior include shattered relationships, unfulfilled dreams, broken hearts, ruined health, and wasted possessions.

Reasons for Prodigal Behavior

The obvious question is, Why? Why would a person so foolishly follow the course of prodigal behavior? Why did it happen in Jesus' day and why does it happen so frequently today?

At the core of prodigal behavior is what the Bible simply and honestly calls "sin." The prophet Jeremiah expressed the essence of sinful behavior so clearly many centuries ago: "The heart is deceitful above all things, and desperately wicked; who can know it?" (Jeremiah 17:9). At its heart, prodigal behavior is essentially sinful, and as such, it is arrogant and self-willed, following the course of Satan himself who authored the initial rebellion against the loving Creator.

Of course, our contemporary culture has come to regard Satan as either a harmless caricature (as in comedian Flip Wilson's gag line, "The debil made me do it!") or a horror movie character. The Bible, however, records his true history and character. He is a rebellious angel whose outright questioning of God's motives toward Eve and

Adam prompted the woman to take the forbidden fruit and offer it to her husband. It was Satan who unsuccessfully tempted Jesus to follow a prodigal course during a time of intense testing early in Jesus' ministry. In fact, so deadly is his intent in opposing God's plan for human life that the Bible refers to him as a man-eating lion seeking to devour individuals who stray from the path of right standards.

Significance and Entitlement

There are two major tools at the disposal of the tempter in his quest to promote prodigal behavior. They are *significance* and *entitlement*.

Because of feelings of inferiority shared by just about every human on planet earth, the desire for significance is often at the heart of prodigal behavior. Entitlement also plays a key role because in our present culture we have bought into the notion that we are entitled to more than we have and that we must pursue that to which we are entitled in order to find happiness.

Entitlement programs, such as Medicaid, Aid to Families with Dependent Children, food stamps, and welfare—things our country has decreed its citizens are entitled to—are a fairly recent invention of our federal government. However, *feeling entitled* has been a part of the human condition ever since that first family acted out their feelings of entitlement to the forbidden fruit in the garden of Eden.

The apostle John, nearing the close of his lengthy tenure of service as a first-century Christian leader, wrote to oppressed believers to explain what life in fellowship with God is really like. In his letter, he cautioned his readers, "Do not love the world or the things in the world" (1 John 2:15). While we do not believe "worldliness" can simply be reduced to a list of "dos and don'ts," (what some Christians half-jokingly call the "dirty dozen" or the "filthy five"), it is worth noting how John elaborates on his warning against falling in love with a system organized by Satan against God (1 John 5:19). He includes three expressions of worldliness which are driven by human desire and which express themselves in prodigal behavior, actions designed to compensate for feelings of inferiority in the drive for significance and to secure that to which one feels entitled.

The first of these, described by John as "the lust of the flesh," is all too frequently seen in our society in the form of *sexual temptation*. While such temptation existed even in the Victorian era, today's society has literally been permeated with the consequences of a generation raised on the notion that everyone is entitled to sexual expression in whatever way he or she wishes. For Phyllis, who chose to become sexually active as a teenager (that's the modern euphemism for immoral behavior), and for Calvin who chose to "get involved" (another euphemism), sexual sin was the choice. The Bible makes it clear that the sexual expression between husband and wife in marriage is legitimate and pleasurable; sexual behavior outside marriage, however, cheapens and degrades God's gift of sexuality and is one type of prodigal behavior (Hebrews 13:4). As AIDS and other sexually transmitted diseases have demonstrated, there are some severe physical consequences to promiscuous behavior. What are less recognized, however, are the damaging emotional and spiritual consequences as well (1 Corinthians 6:13–19).

A second form of prodigal behavior which flows out of feelings of inferiority is what John described as "the lust of the eyes." Today we might refer to this as *materialism* or, more popularly, the desire to purchase everything in sight. Our society has come to laugh about bumper stickers like "A woman's place is in the mall," "Shop 'til you drop," or "My wife has just been inducted into the MasterCard hall of fame." Yet an increasing number of people in our society find themselves filing for bankruptcy, and some seriously consider trying to pay their Visa bill with their MasterCard. When the fancy cars, expensive furniture, boats, and large-screen television sets begin to be repossessed, it becomes clear that materialism is just another dead-end street.

In the first century the apostle Paul urged his associate named Timothy to follow a formula for material balance expressed in the words, "Now godliness with contentment is great gain" (1 Timothy 6:6). One's spiritual well-being and a sense of contentment are far more valuable than trying to "get ahead" materially. Paul also warned those who lust after more money and possessions to be aware of the pain and heartache such pursuits would produce (vv. 9–10). Furthermore, those who are financially well-off shouldn't trust in wealth but should rather submit in trust to the living God who provides for all our needs (vv. 17–18).

Subtle Prodigalism

While the first two examples of prodigal behavior cited by the apostle John are generally easy to spot, the third is perhaps a bit more subtle. The difference can be noted in the label John suggested for it, *the pride of life.* This third avenue begins with arrogant pride and often ends in power struggles, turf wars, and interpersonal conflicts. The Bible also describes these as "wars and fights [which] come from . . .

desires for pleasure that war in your members" (James 4:1). At the root
of these conflicts and struggles is a desire for personal possessions,
control, and prestige—described as "friendship with the world"—and
a heart of jealous pride (James 4:2–6, 10). Sadly, our world today has
become preoccupied with learning how to "swim with the sharks
without being eaten" or discovering the "leadership secrets of Attila
the Hun," all in the name of becoming more skilled at power, control,
and influence.

Furthermore, in all three areas of prodigalism identified by John,
prodigalism can be either subtle or overt, blatant or creeping. Blatant
and overt, we find it easy to identify; however, the subtle or creeping
forms can be just as prodigal. For example, while it's easy to identify as
"prodigal" the woman who earns a living as a high-priced "call girl" or
the drug dealer who distributes cocaine, the Wall Street investment
banker wearing an Armani suit, who defrauds investors of millions of
dollars, is just as guilty of prodigalism based on God's moral inventory.
Likewise, it's easy to see the prodigal character of a televangelist who
frequents a prostitute; yet the televangelist who solicits contributions
to bankroll a lavish lifestyle while callously indifferent to the real needs
of people is just as prodigal as the sexually immoral person.

The New Testament prodigal that Jesus described, perhaps feeling
inferior, desiring to prove his personal significance (since he was the
younger of two brothers), and probably feeling entitled to what he
considered his rightful inheritance, found himself following all three of
the behaviors warned against in John's first-century letter—illegitimate
sexual gratification, blinding materialism, and selfish power-seeking.

Certainly it must have been a calloused pride that motivated him to
do what was unthinkable in the culture of his day—to insist that his
father give him the inheritance that would rightfully become his only
upon his father's death. In effect, what he was saying was *my personal
significance matters more than your life*. In a society in which respect for
parents in general and especially for fathers was the norm, this young
man's request must have jolted Jesus' listeners.

For more than fifteen years, Kenneth Bailey talked to people of oriental
cultures about the implications of the son's request for his inheritance
while his father was still living.[2] He questioned individuals from all walks
of life, from Morocco to India, from Turkey to the Sudan. Over and over
he asked, "Has anyone ever made such a request in your village?"

The response was universally the same: "Never." Such a request
was impossible, and if someone did dare make such a demand, his
father would surely beat him. Why? Bailey was told that such a request
would mean the young man in question wanted his father to die.

This New Testament prodigal not only wanted the father to designate his portion of the inheritance but also to allow him to dispose of the assets in whatever way he pleased. This request illuminated the young man's materialistic motivations. Taking his portion of the inheritance, he became the consummate consumer, wasting what should have provided for the rest of his father's life as well as for his own future security as he enjoyed the fickle pleasures of the present.

Certainly, the caustic accusation of the older brother given later in the story—that the young man had squandered his substance with prostitutes—sounds right on the mark.

Prodigals Today

Both of us spend a significant amount of time traveling in planes. Some time ago on a flight to Houston, Texas, we found ourselves seated next to a sharply dressed young lady—we'll call her Nancy. From her "dress for success" clothing to her alligator briefcase and her stylish hairdo, Nancy radiated the look of modern yuppie success. Yet, in the conversation that took place during the flight, Nancy admitted that her life, although appearing impressive on the outside, was crumbling on the inside. It seems she had fallen into all three of the traps that the Bible identifies as worldly or prodigal behavior.

Early in the conversation, Nancy let it be known that having the nicest material things was important to her. She owned a spacious condo in Houston and drove a Porsche 911—a black one, she explained, because they look the richest. She was the proud possessor of two gold credit cards, American Express and MasterCard. Furthermore, she had just returned from a vacation at one of Mexico's prominent beach resorts, and she was beginning to salt away some of her nearly six-figure income into what she considered the appropriate investments.

However, Nancy wasn't happy. As we talked, she expressed anger toward her boss, the executive vice president of the corporation where she worked. As she put it, "It's a dog-eat-dog world, and I intend to do whatever it takes to become the CEO of this company or some other one. After all, I have just as much ability as my boss or our CEO—probably more."

Not long after admitting to her pride and power struggles, Nancy acknowledged that she had recently broken off a fairly lengthy affair with her boss. She had become quite bitter toward him for refusing to leave his wife for her and expressed feelings of both anger and guilt over a relationship that had hurt rather than helped her climb to the top of the career ladder—her ultimate life goal.

Sadly, although Nancy listened attentively as we shared an alternative to the prodigal path she was following, she chose not to respond to the loving heavenly Father who sent His Son to provide her with forgiveness for sin and could empower a new and godly lifestyle. She left the plane that day, still trusting in materialism, sensuality, and professional power plays as the keys to fulfillment.

It seems Rembrandt himself lived out in some measure the prodigal path which he captured on canvas near the close of his life. His biographers described him as a proud young man, convinced of his own genius, enjoying a luxurious lifestyle, and exhibiting a distinct lack of sensitivity toward those around him. During his late twenties and early thirties, Rembrandt painted a number of self-portraits in lavish costumes, decked out in gold and chains. At the age of thirty, he painted himself and his wife in a brothel, apparently one in Amsterdam's infamous red-light district.

Yet his early success ultimately led to personal grief, financial misfortune, and even bankruptcy. The two decades that followed his financial ruin led to the final two paintings of his life. One showed the prodigal son kneeling in repentance before his loving father. The other portrayed Simeon, the godly old man who had been eagerly awaiting the promised Messiah and who lovingly cradled the infant Jesus to his chest when Mary and Joseph brought Him to the temple. Perhaps Rembrandt was expressing his own return to the loving Father and His Son from the prodigal behavior and personal failures that marked much of his own life.

God's Loving Pull

While the earthly father in Jesus' story was helpless to bring about his son's return, the sovereign heavenly Father knows just how to work on prodigals. He lovingly uses consequences, conflicts, and failures to prompt those of us who follow the prodigal path to face spiritual reality, to turn toward Him when we reach the end of our hoarded resources, and to look toward the light when the darkness grows greatest. Time after time we have seen God graciously allow the lives of a Nancy, a Calvin, a Phyllis, a Dean, or a Marcy to experience the difficult events that box us into a corner where the only way out is to look up to Him.

Breaking Through Denial

Ultimately for each prodigal, just as for the young man of the New Testament, there must come a moment of truth, a point of facing reality, as we shall see later in the book. Each must, as Jesus put it, come to know "the truth, and the truth shall make you free" (John 8:32). Each must turn from flawed ideals and fruitless pursuits to the only Person who in Himself is the Way, the Truth and the Life (John 14:6) In a spiritually thirsty world, Jesus is truly the water of life. For all of us who have been or who are prodigals, He is the Savior who died to pay for our sins, who lovingly intercedes for us before God the Father, and who freely extends to us God's love, grace, and forgiveness.

Endnotes

1. *Webster's New World Dictionary of the American Language* (New York: World Publishing Company, 1963), 375.
2. Kenneth E. Bailey, *Through Peasant Eyes: A Literary-Cultural Approach to the Parables* (Grand Rapids: William B. Eerdmans Publishing Company, 1983), 161–62.

PART ONE

The Parable of the Prodigal Son

It's an amazing drama. Some have even called it "the greatest short story in the world." It constitutes a significant segment of an extended three-part parable or "teaching story" told by Jesus to listeners who undoubtedly fit both lifestyles—that of the prodigal son and of the elder brother.

In the previous paragraph in Luke's gospel, Jesus had told His audience a story about a wedding feast. Many of the invited guests had refused to respond to the invitation to come. Jesus' listeners clearly understood what He meant when He explained that the host commanded his servant to go quickly into the streets and alleys and bring in those who were poor, blind, and impaired. Holding their heads high in arrogance and stroking their full beards, the Pharisees must have let it be known by their body language how they felt about extending an invitation to those who were so clearly unworthy of God's love. As the tax collectors and sinners—the outcasts of society— drew close to hear Jesus (Luke 15:1), these Pharisees and scribes began to voice their complaints.

Without question, tax collectors and sinners were the kind of people you would expect to include under the umbrella of prodigal behavior— tax collectors (like Levi, one of Jesus' disciples also known as Matthew) sold themselves to Rome in order to secure the right to get rich under the Roman system of tax collection. They were despised alike by religious leaders and common, God-fearing Jews.

The term *sinner* included all the outcasts of society, and the Pharisees used this term for anyone who was not of their persuasion. A good Pharisee held the view that God loved the righteous—specifically him—but hated sinners. In fact, the Pharisees actually believed that God delighted in the death of sinners since this removed them from His presence.[1]

Like any number of religious and social conflicts in our own day, the situation was ripe for a confrontation. Here was Jesus, a respected rabbi in Israel, setting an example in extending loving acceptance to tax collectors and sinners. Outwardly, the religious leaders griped and murmured; inwardly, they must have seethed with indignant rage. They were furious over Jesus' continued association with the kind of people they viewed as incorrigible and totally unworthy of God's love. They angrily interrupted Jesus with their disgusted complaints.

Yet while the Pharisees concentrated their verbal attack on Jesus, they were surrounded by a crowd of the very same people the Pharisees despised! The gospel writer Luke singles out "tax collectors and sinners" as forming the crowd of people eager to listen to Jesus. So Jesus began to present a single parable, which He unfolded in three movements, to show just how far the Pharisees had gone beyond the Old Testament's call for separation from sinful behavior. The evident joy of the characters in each parable—the shepherd (Luke 15:5–6), the housewife (v. 9), and the father (vv. 20–24, 32)—reflected the joy of God Himself toward a repenting sinner.

Each of these three vignettes also demonstrated the diligence with which God pursues the lost—a diligence being modeled before their eyes by the One telling the story. Yet it was not until the third vignette of this parable that the Pharisees' rebellious, arrogant attitude was shown to be just as prodigal as the "sinners" they hated. These Pharisees couldn't help but get the message that their own self-righteous attitudes clearly paralleled the attitude of the older brother.

The story of the lost sheep, of the lost coin, and of the lost son all illustrate the point Jesus would later drive home with vivid clarity, "The Son of Man has come to seek and to save that which was lost" (Luke 19:10).

There is one ironic contrast to be seen in these three stories, however. The coin was lost through no fault of its own. The sheep, a hapless animal, became lost because it aimlessly wandered off into the wilderness.

Sadly, like many today, the son became lost because of his own stubborn, self-willed determination. Unlike the coin or the sheep, he made irresponsible, self-destructive choices that led to his downfall.

---

1. J. Dwight Pentecost, *The Parables of Jesus* (Grand Rapids: Zondervan, 1982), 99.

CHAPTER ONE

"Doing It My Way"

City Lights

The bright array of city lights as far as I can see,
The great white way shines through the night
for lonely guys like me.
A cabaret, a honky-tonk, their flashing signs invite
A broken heart to lose itself in the glow of city lights.

"City Lights," words and music by Bill Anderson. Copyright 1958, TNT Music, Inc., 3110 Climbing Rose, San Antonio, Texas 78230. Copyright renewed. International copyright secured. All rights reserved. Used by permission.

Then He said, "A certain man had two sons. And the younger of them said to his father, 'Father, give me the portion of goods that falls to me.' So he divided to them his livelihood. And not many days after, the younger son gathered all together, journeyed to a far country, and there wasted his possessions with prodigal living." (Luke 15:11–13)

Jesus took this story right from the fabric of first-century life. Undoubtedly His listeners, like many of us today, could identify directly with some element of it or knew some family with a similar experience.

The younger of the two sons longed to be out on his own—to go where he wanted to go and to do what he wanted to do. He was tired of living in his father's house and frustrated by his father's restraints and restrictions. He probably also wanted to get away from his older brother who may have been a frequent critic and the sibling he wished he'd never had.

Perhaps he dreamed of making a fortune on his own. Surely it would be easy for him to find something to do that would be better than the hard, hot work in the fields. His head must have been dizzy with dreams of his coming success.

But he would need money to finance the adventures before him—lots of it—and he had none. Someday he would receive an inheritance which amounted to one-third of his father's possessions. According to the law, his older brother would receive two-thirds. That wouldn't happen until his father died, however; then the inheritance would be divided. The family land, however, would probably never be his for it belonged to the family and was passed on from one generation to another, each time to the oldest son. So he would have to put his plans on hold and be patient, perhaps waiting for years until the death of his father.

This was a young man in a hurry, however. He wanted his inheritance, and he wanted it now!

A Brash Demand

So one day he said, "Father, give me the portion of goods that falls to me." We pick up a hint about his character from the disrespectful way in which he spoke to his father. There was no "please." He didn't include a "thank you." He just said, "Give me." It was a command, not a request; a demand, not a plea. This unreasonable demand must have grieved his father deeply. In essence, he was saying, "I wish you were dead!"

The father didn't have to do what his arrogant son requested. But he did. Apparently he sold a considerable portion of his holdings, converting them to cash and dividing the funds between his two sons.

This father was not weak for capitulating to the demands of his headstrong, wayward son. He knew his son very well. Surely he had tried to teach him how to live an honest, productive life. But he hadn't listened. Now the father felt he must allow his wayward son to follow the natural bent of his heart and discover for himself where it would lead him. He had to learn things the hard way—like the law of "sowing and reaping." One of God's unchangeable laws, like gravity, this "law of the farm" is even recognized by modern business and management experts as governing all areas of life—we get back what we put in. Computer programmers have reduced this principle to the acronym GIGO—"Garbage in, garbage out."[1]

With a big enough bankroll to fulfill his wildest dreams, the young man wasted no time in leaving home. Today we might say that happiness to him was the family farm receding in his rear-view mirror. Showing little or no heart for his family, he packed his bags and burned his bridges. As far as he was concerned, there was nothing back home for him ever to return to. He intended to leave that place forever and show his father and his older brother that he didn't need them. He could make it on his own!

Of course he didn't know what he was getting into. He didn't realize just how inexperienced and immature he was. He had never been through a "too-much-money-in-my-pocket" test. He thought he was smart, but he was sadly deficient in wisdom. He thought he had a handle on his life, but he had little self-control. He thought he could handle his relationships with others, but he was prone to make poor choices in friends. Most important of all, he didn't understand his bent toward evil. Or perhaps he just didn't care.

So he traveled to a distant country, many miles from his home and family. Jesus doesn't identify the young man's destination. More important than where he went, however, was what he did when he got there.

Having It All and Having a Ball

We might expect that once he arrived at his destination, the young man would probably indulge himself a bit—spend a little money foolishly—then invest the rest to insure that he could continue to live at the same standard he was accustomed to.

But that's not what happened. He didn't consult a financial advisor or ask for advice from others. He did no estate planning, he bought no stocks or bonds, and he maintained no bank accounts. He did nothing!

Nothing, that is, except live loosely and wildly. Choose any adjective you want—profligate, extravagant, lavish—all describe the kind of life he chose as soon as he hit town.

This young man was certainly not the only person who ever rushed wastefully through a fortune. A young man nicknamed "Coal-Oil Johnny" Steele reportedly wiped out a two-million-dollar inheritance in just a few years, once spending $8,000 on clothes in a single day. On another occasion he is said to have leased an entire Philadelphia hotel for a night at a cost of over $10,000—just so he could fire a clerk who had not accorded him the deference he demanded.[2]

Another big spender was Diamond Jim Brady, who owned a separate set of jeweled studs, cuff-links, and rings for every day of the month. Reportedly he was in the habit of giving chorus girls a thousand dollars apiece for attending his lavish parties.

Then there was Bobby, the son of a wealthy industrialist. Bobby selected his college on the basis of the parties held on campus. As the dean who dismissed him after his first year told him, ". . . you came to a school planning to major in the good life—and you succeeded in that while you managed to fail every course you signed up for." Bobby had arrived on campus with a fistful of his father's credit cards and actually managed to charge almost $100,000 on clothes, parties, and alcoholic beverages. He also wrecked two new automobiles, including the sports convertible he had been given for his high school graduation. His dad finally woke up to the situation when his son's dismissal from school coincided with Bobby's demand for $1,000—supposedly to pay a personal debt but actually to finance a girlfriend's abortion.

Riches to Rags

However we describe the young son's lifestyle—the lifestyle of the rich and famous or the lifestyle of the rash and foolish—one thing remains certain: he soon went broke.

It doesn't take a financial wizard to figure out that this young man was headed for bankruptcy. He spent his money right and left, and soon he had none left at all. He had squandered all his resources and lost his inheritance. His was not a rags-to-riches story. It was the other way around. He ended up learning that when your outgo exceeds your income, your upkeep will be your downfall!

Now he was deserted, destitute, and discouraged. What a tragedy!

But the tragedy of his dissipated life doesn't even begin to compare with the tragedy of what he did with the gift he had received from God.

The money that he had been given was his inheritance, passed down from his ancestors. It was essentially a gift from God to his tribe, his family. And he had carelessly and foolishly squandered it. Squandering God's gift—no matter what it is—is sin and the essence of the prodigal life.

God expected him to exercise stewardship—the prudent, careful use of one's resources—rather than "squandership." But he failed his stewardship test miserably. He had wanted to be free, to make his own decisions, to run his own life. Instead, he wasted all that God had given him with his wild and reckless living. In reality, what he had looked on as his new-found freedom simply enslaved him to the worst form of bondage—the bondage of sin.

Endnotes

1. Stephen R. Covey, A. Roger Merrill, and Rebecca R. Merrill, *First Things First* (New York: Simon & Schuster, 1994), 56; Sydney N. Bremer, *Spirit of Apollo* (Lexington, NC: Successful Achievement, 1971), 167.

2. Paul Lee Tan, *Encyclopedia of 7700 Illustrations* (Rockville, Maryland: Assurance Publications, 1979), 767.

CHAPTER TWO

The Road to Misery

All the misfortunes of mankind derive from one single thing, which is their inability to be at ease at home.

—Pascal, *Pensées*

Misery acquaints a man with strange bedfellows.

—Shakespeare, *The Tempest*

"And not many days after, the younger son gathered all together, journeyed to a far country, and there wasted his possessions with prodigal living." (Luke 15:13)

During our years in Christian ministry, both of us have had the opportunity to teach in schools where men and women train for vocational Christian service. We have both invested many years in education ourselves, studying in college and in seminary in preparation to teach the Bible.

During that time we have generally encountered two predominant attitudes toward the Bible. Some students personalize it, to their benefit. Others rationalize it, to their harm.

Needless to say, the appropriate attitude toward the Bible is to personalize it, to make it ours. It's clear from the way Jesus addressed His listeners that this was His intention in telling this three-part parable. He didn't simply say, "A man had a sheep," or "A woman lost a coin." Instead, He addressed the crowd specifically with the words, "What man of you . . ." In so doing, He set the tone for each part of this parable. His goal was that they apply it.

Unfortunately, some people simply wish to gain a theoretical or academic understanding of the Bible without allowing it to touch and transform their lives. One such individual, Rob, was overheard telling a friend during the early days of his first tenure as pastor of a church, "You really ought to go into this. It's a great racket. People are so gullible." Ironically, Rob eventually found himself facing personal disgrace and even legal action as a result of his attitude toward his congregation.

Then there was Doug. A gifted communicator, he was appointed to pastor a church early in his seminary training. However, his own life and the lives of many to whom he ministered were scarred because of Doug's uncontrolled sexual appetite which was acted out toward unsuspecting young females in both his church and the school he attended.

Richard and Nellie had been active for years in their church. Both had taught Sunday school, worked with young people, and otherwise carried on a public ministry. When their pastor suggested that all those who taught would benefit from a special time set aside for spiritual emphasis and to polish teaching skills, their reply was, "We don't need it, but we'll attend anyway, if you insist." Their friends were totally shocked when their public facade of godliness eventually collapsed in marital violence.

Since Jesus hoped His listeners would personalize the story, we want to restate the obvious. It is our desire that everyone who reads this book will personalize the account of the prodigal, not only hearing what the Bible says and understanding what it means, but also applying its truths to your own life.

The Younger Son

For many readers this may mean identifying with the younger of the two sons. Simply put, he was ready to be on his own. He wanted to go wherever his desires took him, do whatever his heart desired, and enjoy that to which he felt entitled.

In first-century society, sons were considered a special blessing in a family and were more highly prized than daughters. One reason was obvious: a son could carry on the family name. In addition, sons were workers, helping with the family farm or business. Furthermore, in all likelihood, sons would be able to care for their aging parents when they were beyond the point of providing for themselves. In fact, the responsibilities of adult sons in biblical times included providing support for their parents when they became old and giving them a proper burial when they died.[1]

In return for fulfilling these responsibilities, the oldest son could also anticipate receiving a significant reward. Typically, the inheritance was divided among the heirs at the death of the father, and the firstborn son received a double portion of the inheritance (Deuteronomy 21:17). When the Old Testament king Jehoshaphat died, all his sons inherited silver, gold, and precious jewels, plus responsibility for the fortified cities. The kingdom, however, went to his firstborn son, Jehoram (2 Chronicles 21:1–3).

No doubt the younger son was keenly aware of the fact that his brother was to receive both a larger inheritance and continued authority when his father died. Maybe he was suspicious that things might actually be worse for him then. Perhaps the father had not pushed this younger son to work hard and be responsible. As a result, the younger son may have suspected that his older brother would be harder on him than their dad had been.

Perhaps he dreamed of succeeding on his own, of gaining fame and fortune. Apparently his father, like most of the people of that day, farmed the fields. Anyone who has farmed knows how hard such work can be. Perhaps the young man even considered such labor demeaning. Surely there must be something better for him!

Whatever the case, he clearly didn't consider his own responsibility to care for his father throughout his older years and to give him a proper burial. The traditions that had been handed down since the days of his Old Testament ancestors meant nothing to him.

In our society, people sometimes give power of attorney to an adult child to manage their affairs, or they give large monetary gifts to their children before they die in order to avoid inheritance taxes. Therefore, the incredible arrogance of this young man's action may escape us. It is clear that this son didn't want his father's protective oversight, didn't consider his father's counsel important, and totally devalued the responsibility to care for his father.

Of course, the desire to leave home is a very natural part of the growing up process. In recent years, both of us have experienced "an empty nest" as one and then another of our children have moved out. Some of them have married, others have pursued college and career opportunities. None, however, has requested his or her share of either the Kroll or Hawkins family estate (not that there is any great sum in either estate to be requested!).

So the fault of this young man lies not in his desire to leave home but rather in his callous rejection of his father's authority, protection, counsel, and of his own responsibility. We are not told about the mother in this story—perhaps she had died—but if she were a part of the story, apparently this young man would have had just as little regard for her as he did for his father.

Similarities with Today

In many respects the first century prodigal described by Jesus bears a remarkable similarity to the typical baby boomer or buster of our day. Surveys conducted by the Barna Research Group show more than sixty percent of Americans have a characteristically "self-centered, experiential view of life." Barna describes Americans as struggling and searching, seeking adventure and fulfillment, engineering rapid shifts in values and behaviors. This description remarkably parallels the career of the young man following his departure from his father. Barna notes that "denial of sin is rampant in America." He observes that we have just come through the want and selfishness of the "me decade" of the 1980s and have now entered a decade where priorities and personal faith are once again becoming important to more and more individuals.[2]

If these assessments are accurate, then the story of the prodigal son and other biblical prodigals can shed significant light on the struggle of many contemporary prodigals, directing them back to a Father who cares and who provides the only ultimate source of meaning and purpose in life. Certainly our contemporary society is filled with brash young men and women who want their inheritance in life and who want it now, just as the first-century prodigal did.

Jesus' description of the encounter in which the young man expressed his demands to his father reads as tersely as one of those capsule stories found on the front page of *USA Today*. There is no in-depth explanation of whether the young man had been brooding over this encounter or that the father had been fearing such an exchange, although both seem likely.

Lessons for Dads

To be sure, the Bible doesn't tell us the details of how this father raised his son. However, most Jewish fathers of his day, in contrast to many dads in our society, took seriously the mandate of the Mosaic Law to instill character traits like respect, honesty, and reverence for God by teaching the Law on a consistent basis (Deuteronomy 6:4–9). So it seems reasonable to suppose this father had communicated these important values to his son and had exercised loving discipline when it was needed.

Yet clearly something had gone wrong in the relationship. While this isn't the main point of the story, there are two important principles for us to draw from the situation. First, there can be no doubt about the importance of fathers investing time in their sons. Far too many of today's fathers have become workaholics, almost prisoners of their jobs, to the detriment of their homes and families. Far too few dads are willing to invest the necessary time for success in family life. Both of our fathers did, even though they worked hard. Each would sit down with us on a daily basis, Bible in hand, to teach God's principles.

A second lesson we need to remember is that every person has the freedom to respond or not respond to God's truth. Although spending time communicating personal love and biblical principles to children can certainly help ensure that they will become mature, godly adults, it is not an ironclad guarantee. In the Old Testament book of Proverbs, a familiar verse states, "Train up a child in the way he should go, and when he is old he will not depart from it" (Proverbs 22:6). It's not a promise that every child so trained will never deviate from the straight and narrow. Rather, it's a proverb, a general statement of truth. The proverb encourages parents to recognize their children's individual personalities, guide them in pursuing their natural personality bent, and motivate them to develop an appetite for spiritual truth.

The bottom line is that this process seems to have had little impact upon the spiritual life of the younger son. His natural bent was to pursue the desires of his own heart, and he opted not to listen to his father. This dad chose the option of "tough love" and allowed his son to learn life's lessons the hard way. How much better off we are when we willingly listen to the wise counsel of others rather than insisting that we learn life's hard lessons ourselves! Unfortunately, it's not a new phenomenon.

The Rehoboam Factor

The story is told in the Old Testament of a man whose father was a great king. Many have called his father the wisest man who ever lived.

One would think growing up in the home of Solomon, the man who wrote several thousand proverbs, would ensure that one would become a wise son who paid attention to his father. Yet the Bible records that Rehoboam followed just the opposite course shortly after his father's death. Rehoboam was about to be crowned king when a delegation from the tribes of Israel requested a lower tax rate to support the government. In return they promised personal loyalty and service (1 Kings 12:1–4).

King Rehoboam consulted with the older men who had advised his father, Solomon. They replied with a principle still true today: a leader who is a servant to those he leads promotes a loyal, long-term following (vv. 5–7).

Sadly, Rehoboam abandoned the counsel of the mature advisors and consulted with his contemporaries, who were much younger. Taking their advice, he responded to the delegation with a notable lack of graciousness, arrogantly asserting in the proverbial expression, "My little finger shall be thicker than my father's waist!" (vv. 8–11). His harsh answer ultimately precipitated the division of Israel into a northern and southern kingdom and resulted in the declining influence of the royal line of David and Solomon.

Rehoboam provided living proof of the principle that every person has the freedom to respond or not respond to the truth. Even though he heard the truth from his father, Rehoboam chose to refuse the wise counsel of older men. This "Rehoboam factor," which leads to learning things the hard way, seems to have infected the New Testament prodigal as well as many of today's contemporary prodigals.

Life on His Own

Showing little regard for his family, the prodigal hastily packed his bags, gathered all his possessions, and left home, apparently intent on never returning to his family. Life on the farm had no attraction for him. A distant country—probably a big city—was where his imagination would carry him.

He certainly showed very little instinct for business or for his own future security. A thinking person would have undoubtedly invested a portion of his capital in his home area where he was known. After all, first-century travelers were at risk of robbery (Jesus described such an event in His parable of the Good Samaritan in Luke 10:30–37). Plus, he stood to lose the rest of his inheritance in unprofitable investments or bad financial decisions—he simply took all his liquid assets along with him and left home, bankroll in hand, to fulfill his wildest dreams. His plan was simply to put as much distance as possible between himself and the farm where he had grown up. He'd show his father and that irritating older brother that he didn't need them—he was perfectly capable of making it on his own.

Ironically, material possessions provide one of the ultimate tests of personal maturity and spiritual vitality. In his letter to first-century Christians, James (the stepbrother of Jesus and leader of the church in Jerusalem) encourages the poorer individual to rejoice in his spiritual success and the wealthier person to consider his possible financial decline since riches fade like flowers or grass in the burning sun (James 1:9–11). His warning is consistent with the Bible's other instructions: those who are wealthy should not be arrogant or high-minded, should not rely upon wealth which is never dependable, but should rather trust the living God who gives us the wealth we enjoy. Those who have been entrusted with material wealth are to practice good stewardship by engaging in good deeds, by giving generously and willingly, by making wise investments to protect against the future, and by making the spiritual rather than the material their priority in life (1 Timothy 6:17–19).

No doubt his father had explained similar principles to him (many are found in the Old Testament book of Proverbs), but he had chosen to ignore them. Jesus mentioned no examples of his investing for the future, managing his cash prudently, or giving to the needy. Instead, Jesus simply states that the young man set off for a distant country to squander his wealth in wild living.

Bright Lights, Big City

Where would a young man looking for a good time head? Rome, the capital of the empire, might seem to be the natural place to seek fame and fortune. The Greek city of Corinth was notorious in the first century for its party atmosphere. Egypt, bustling with foreign trade and travelers, was always an exciting stop.

In all likelihood, he headed for some urban area where he could lose himself in the glitz and glamour of the big city, where every kind of want and pleasure imaginable could be purchased for a price. And he certainly had the money to pay for it all. Soon he discovered the principle expressed in a seventies rock song of having "all the friends that money could buy." And when the money was gone, so were the friends.

Both of us have visited some of the large cities of the world: Rome, London, Athens, New York City, Los Angeles, and others. While those cities can present a gleaming, pristine image, each has a seamier side, a side that welcomes young prodigals, turns their lives inside out, and leaves them stripped of values, virtue, morals, money, and even hope itself.

Jana was an eighteen-year-old, talented in music and the arts. She was fed up with the strict religious upbringing imposed by her parents. After a series of confrontations with her mother over curfew, she withdrew the savings her parents had helped her amass for education at a Christian college, packed her bags, and caught the next Greyhound for New York City. Certain she would wind up in Broadway stardom in a short time, Jana found herself robbed of her resources, raped, and ultimately forced into the shameful degradation of street prostitution. When her father finally located her six weeks after her departure from home, she had a heavy drug habit, a pimp who viewed her as simply a source of income, and a filthy, third-story walk-up apartment where she took her customers.

As she put it later, "I was both lucky and blessed. A lot of people didn't get out alive of what I'd gotten into."

By her own admission, Jana had expected to arrive in New York and begin to experience a lifestyle like the television shows she had seen, the lifestyle of the rich and famous. Instead she fell into the lifestyle of the rash and foolish.

That's exactly what happened with the young prodigal of the first century. Seeking a luxurious and easy lifestyle, he wound up becoming a reckless consumer, spending like there was no tomorrow.

Nest Egg Depleted

What he thought was an inexhaustible financial well soon ran dry. Like many people today, he quickly found himself bankrupt, his resources all squandered, and his inheritance gone for good. The one thing he didn't have, which has helped many in our society go through their resources even more quickly, was that incredible piece of plastic by which many a fool and his money have been rapidly parted—the all-too-common credit card.

Bettye Banks, a financial counselor for many years with Consumer

Credit Counseling Service, tells of a couple she counseled who had been fairly well-off financially but who had fallen into the credit card trap. "These individuals had over nineteen credit cards—Visa, MasterCard, major department stores—you name it, they had it. When we took stock of where they were financially, their annual income was just under $30,000 but their installment debt on credit cards (not including automobiles or the house) totaled well over $100,000! That's bankrupt with a capital B."

Sadly Bettye explains, "As a believer, I'm sorry to say I've seen this happen to many Christians. It's so easy to spend more than you have these days. Credit cards certainly contribute, but it's almost as though there is an attitude of 'I'm entitled to have all this right now.' We especially see it in the young families with two incomes and no children. They often don't realize how easy it is to spend more than is available. This same risk is present, perhaps even greater, for single adults, especially those who leave home with their first credit card in hand, ready to take on the world. Unfortunately, many of them should have refused to listen to the commercial that suggests, 'Don't leave home without it.' They would have been far better off if they had."

Gary Purdy and Bill Campbell have many years of experience as financial consultants with the investment firm of Smith Barney. They have talked with numerous individuals who have received a lump sum settlement from a job change or an inheritance. What could have provided them with a measure of financial security for their future, not to mention resources that could have helped support God's work, was quickly spent. "It's sad," Gary commented after he returned from an extended missions trip with Campus Crusade to the former Soviet Union. "There are so many people who could have provided for their own future and at the same time supported people in God's work who are living on a fraction of what they need. Instead, all they did was spend it."

Money and Virtue

It's been suggested that virtue and prosperity often have trouble living together. This is clearly evident in the prodigal's experience. Never is it more essential that we exercise the virtue of self-control than in times of prosperity. The prodigal's wild fling was marked by anything but discipline or self-control. Perhaps he engaged in the kind of lifestyle so often glamorized in Hollywood movies, television dramas, and in modern novels, sampling all the pleasures life had to offer. In our own time, he would have been a good candidate for a front page story in the *National Enquirer* or some other supermarket newspaper.

Apparently he didn't realize what a rude awakening he was in for. For a while he had all the pleasures money could buy—then they were gone. The friends, who were attracted to easy money like bees to a flower garden, were gone. Where once there had been nonstop partying like a beach filled with college kids celebrating spring break, now there was only the sound of silence. Jesus' terse description, recorded by Luke, was that he "wasted his possessions with prodigal living. But when he had spent all, there arose a severe famine in that land; and he began to be in want" (vv. 13–14). Suddenly the young man was deserted, destitute, discouraged, and broke.

Two Ways to Lose

There are two ways we can lose our financial security. One way is through no fault of our own, the kind of circumstances financial experts today refer to as "a downturn in the economy" resulting from "market forces." It's not very comforting to be the victim of "market forces," but it's understandable. The other way is by the kind of careless irresponsibility shown by the first-century prodigal.

Sadly, this young man learned the lesson expressed in a poem by Thomas Gray, which is the source of one of our most common expressions:

> Not all that tempts your wand'ring eyes
> And heedless hearts, is lawful prize;
> Nor all, that glisters, gold.[3]

The glittering lifestyle that seemed so fulfilling turned out to be only so much fool's gold. With his friends and his money gone and his family long ago abandoned, he must have felt very alone—but he really wasn't. God was lovingly watching over him, even guiding the steps of his life so as to ultimately draw him lovingly back toward home where he belonged. But as we shall see in the next chapter, the circumstances God brought into his life initially seemed anything at all but loving.

Endnotes

1. J. I. Packer, Merrill C. Tenney, and William White Jr., *The Bible Almanac* (Nashville: Thomas Nelson, 1980), 413.
2. George Barna, *The Barna Report 1992–93* (Ventura: Regal Books, 1992), 36.
3. From *Ode on the Death of a Favorite Cat* by Thomas Gray, 1747.

CHAPTER THREE

Life at the Bottom

I Threw It All Away

Once I had mountains in the palm of my hand,
and rivers that ran through every day.
I must have been mad, I never knew what I had,
until I threw it all away.
Love is all there is, it makes the world go round.
Love and only love, it can't be denied.
No matter what you think about it,
you just won't be able to do without it.
Take a tip from one who's tried.

---

*But when he had spent all, there arose a severe famine in that land,
and he began to be in want. Then he went and joined himself to a
citizen of that country, and he sent him into his fields to feed swine. And
he would gladly have filled his stomach with the pods that the swine ate,
and no one gave him anything.* (Luke 15:14–16)

Have you ever noticed how disasters, personal and otherwise, often
seem to run in twos or threes or even more? A friend of ours who lives
in Los Angeles recently lamented how residents there experienced
multiple disaster—riots followed by fires, then floods, and finally a
massive earthquake. "It's almost like the Four Horsemen of the
Apocalypse decided to make us their focal point," he concluded.

Perhaps that's how the young man felt when two disasters struck
his life almost simultaneously. The first—the depletion of all his
financial resources—he was personally responsible for. The second
was one over which he had no control, and it happened very soon after
his money was gone. A severe famine struck his newly-chosen country.

Suddenly the young man faced a double dilemma—no funds and an
intense famine. What was he to do? How would he eat?

In recent days both of us have seen firsthand the homeless, hungry
people who crowd the streets of cities like Los Angeles and New York.
Wherever we live, most of us have seen homeless, unkempt people
standing at busy street corners holding up crudely crafted cardboard
signs saying, "Homeless . . . will work for food." Perhaps that's where
the young man of our story found himself as he faced one disaster
multiplied by another disaster.

Famine in the Land

Famines were a common occurrence in the Middle East in biblical
times. In the book of Genesis, Abraham left the land of Canaan to
travel to Egypt because of a famine. A three-year famine occurred
during the latter years of King David, and a severe famine struck the
city of Samaria during the days of the infamous King Ahab. This
famine was so severe one of the women of the city came to the king to
complain that she and a neighbor had agreed they would eat her son
one day and the neighbor's son the next, but the neighbor had hidden
her son (2 Kings 6:26–29). Such graphic language and inhumane
circumstances illustrate the severe impact of biblical famines.

The New Testament records a "great famine throughout all the
world" during the reign of Claudius Caesar around A.D. 46 (Acts
11:28). In the Gospels Jesus warned of recurring famines throughout

the world. Such famines can be triggered by natural causes, such as droughts, excessive rain, floods, or extremely cold weather. Other factors may include insect plagues or plant diseases. War is frequently a major factor in famine. Twenty-seven million people are said to have starved to death following World War I.[1]

Jesus' terse description gives no detail other than that the famine was severe. It covered the entire country and created a crisis for the hungry and homeless young man. As we noted earlier, Jesus didn't give the location of the city in which the young prodigal experienced a famine. However, we suspect that it was outside Jewish territory since the young man found himself a job that no self-respecting Jewish young man would take—feeding pigs. Perhaps the far country to which he had fled was east of the Sea of Galilee where non-Jewish farmers raised pigs (see Luke 8:26–37).

In these circumstances we can see clearly the timing of God—getting this young man's attention and causing him to remember just how well-off he had been in his father's home. It's apparent God placed him in this famine-stricken country at just the right time and in a way designed to have the most definite and dramatic impact.

God's Timing

God's timing in such things can be seen throughout the Bible. Many people are familiar with the Old Testament story of Joseph who was sold as a slave by his brothers. It's not only a familiar event from the book of Genesis but was even taken to the Broadway stage in *Joseph's Amazing Technicolor Dream Coat.*

Joseph ended up in Egypt where, despite human injustice and interference, God caused him to rise from the rank of prisoner to the second-highest position in the mightiest nation on earth at the time. A few years later a famine struck Palestine and threatened to extinguish the chosen family line of Abraham, Isaac, and Joseph's father, Jacob. As prime minister of Egypt, Joseph was in a position to provide for his brothers and their families—and extend to them the hand of forgiveness—when they were forced to come to him for food.

God's perfect timing can also be seen later in Israel's history in the Old Testament. The Jewish nation had been conquered, and many Jews were taken as exiles to Persia. There a Persian official named Haman jealously plotted to exterminate God's chosen people. But God had prepared a young Jewish girl named Esther to become queen of the Persian empire even though King Xerxes was unaware of her racial heritage.

Even though the name of God never appears in the book of Esther, His divine protection can be seen in the incredible timing of circumstances that ultimately led to the reversal of Haman's Hitler-like attempt to wipe out the Jewish people.

God was not surprised by the prodigal's circumstances—far from home, flat broke, utterly helpless. His party-loving buddies had disappeared. He was without friends, funds, or food, with no one to turn to—which is exactly where God wanted him to be.

One thing he could do was swallow his pride and return home. It seems at first that he gave this option little or no consideration. He may have been broke, but he was not yet broken. He didn't need his father or family, nor did it cross his mind that he needed to return, make apologies for the shabby way he had treated his father, and restore the broken relationships with God and the people who mattered in his life. No, he wasn't ready to admit that he had been wrong, nor was God anywhere in his picture or his plans.

Living in Denial

It's incredible how persistently this young man maintained his facade. His fortune was gone, famine gripped the land—and he thought all he needed was a job! Yet this kind of denial is quite common today. It prompts an alcoholic to say, "I just need to cut back a little on my drinking—and it would help if I had a drink right now to help me think about how to cut back."

During a severe famine, a job wasn't easy to come by. Until now this young man had demonstrated no propensity for work. About the only asset he had to list on his résumé might have been that he was the son of a wealthy landowner in a distant country. That probably wouldn't count for much.

How ironic that he wound up on a farm feeding pigs! It's almost as if we can see God's sense of humor as the story unfolds. Here was a young man who wanted nothing to do with the work of his father's farm, yet he winds up working on a farm in a foreign land. He had left home to free himself from dependence on his father; now he found himself totally dependent on a stranger. Furthermore, though there was plenty of food in his father's home, the only food that came his way was meant for the pigs.

Feeding and caring for these creatures must have been dirty, distasteful, and humiliating. After all, no animal was considered quite as unclean to a Jew as a pig—although a dog may have been close. Jews regarded pigs with revulsion. The ultimate act of desecration in

Jewish history happened in 167 B.C. when a pagan conqueror sacrificed a sow on the altar of the temple in Jerusalem.

So, like the starving outcasts in India surrounded by sacred cows they can neither kill nor eat, here was a young man surrounded by animals forbidden as food by Jewish dietary laws (Leviticus 11:7). Not only was he now faced with hard work and personal humiliation, his situation was compounded by his constant hunger. One would normally expect that the farmer who hired the young man would see to it that he had food to eat, but evidently this was not the case. The young man's stomach must have been growling, and he was tempted to fill his empty belly with the husks he was feeding the pigs—but he couldn't bring himself to do it.

These were not the corn husks that are typically used to feed pigs in North America. Rather they were the dark brown, horn-shaped pods of the carob tree, flattened to resemble a dried banana. Sometimes referred to as "the poor man's chocolate," these pods contained a sweet-tasting, gelatinous substance inside and were frequently used to feed the poorer classes of people in the ancient Near East as well as the livestock. A Jewish rabbi once wrote that "when Israel is reduced to the carob tree, then they become repentant."

Apparently that's what it took for this young Jewish man to come to his senses. He could have grown bitter toward his father, bitter toward his circumstances, and even bitter toward God. After all, the message his employer was giving him was as inescapable as the odor from the pigsty—the livestock were more important than his life. He was of lesser importance than the pigs he cared for! Nothing could have been more humiliating to a young man of Jewish origin who had started off with such great promise and resources.

God wasn't being harsh or unfair with him. He was simply using the consequences of the prodigal's foolish choices to get his attention. Several years ago, the manufacturer of a well-known brand of oil filters produced a television commercial featuring an actor portraying a mechanic in grease-stained clothing. Standing in front of an automobile where the engine was obviously being replaced, the mechanic held the advertiser's brand of oil filter and reminded viewers, "You can pay me now or pay me later."

The message of that commercial perfectly compliments the painful lesson learned by the prodigal. Whether the issue is regular oil change and filter replacement to protect the engine of the family car or making important life decisions, neglecting the discipline of right choices will ultimately produce serious consequences.

So far, this undisciplined young man had been content to live just for himself and for the moment. He desperately needed what the Bible refers to as *repentance*—that change of mind that ultimately leads to a change of life. C. S. Lewis, in his classic *The Problem of Pain*, pointed out that pain insists on being attended to. "God whispers to us in our pleasures, speaks in our conscience and shouts in our pain. It is His megaphone to rouse a deaf world." [2]

For the young prodigal, the volume had risen to deafening levels. But this time the message was from God, and the prodigal was finally ready to face the music and begin to think.

Endnotes

1. Paul Lee Tan, *Encyclopedia of 7700 Illustrations* (Rockville, Maryland: Assurance Publications, 1979), 420–421.

2. C. S. Lewis, *The Problem of Pain* (New York: The MacMillian Co., 1940).

CHAPTER FOUR

The Process That Leads to Change

The fault, dear Brutus, is not in our stars, but in ourselves.

—Shakespeare, *Julius Caesar*

But when he came to himself, he said, "How many of my father's hired servants have bread enough and to spare, and I perish with hunger! I will arise and go to my father, and will say to him, 'Father, I have sinned against heaven and before you, and I am no longer worthy to be called your son. Make me like one of your hired servants.'" (Luke 15:17–19)

We've all heard the old Chinese proverb that says a journey of a thousand miles begins with a single step. For this miserable young prodigal, life had brought him to the place where he was almost ready to take that first step—a journey back to his father that must have seemed like a thousand-mile walk no matter what the actual distance may have been.

Yet before the young man could move in the right direction, a process had to take place in his heart to produce repentance and a changed life. Jesus described this experience to a group of self-righteous listeners when He said, "You shall know the truth, and the truth shall make you free" (John 8:32). This process begins with knowledge, focuses on the truth, and leads to freedom.

It is possible this young man had never in his entire life engaged in the discipline of serious thought. Maybe he had just reacted to circumstances and taken the easy way out. Perhaps he had never been challenged to think. His father or even his older brother may have done his thinking for him. Certainly he hadn't been thinking when he decided to leave home or when he confronted his father, gathered his inheritance, and left home to pursue his own self-centered happiness.

Why had it all fallen apart? He must have felt incredibly hopeless as he stood in the pigsty, perhaps in the heat of summer, and fed the pigs. Hunger gnawed at his stomach, and loneliness filled his heart. He finally began to recall just how good things had been back home. *How stupid I've been. How thoughtless; I figured my life would be so much better than it was at home. But it's worse. I never dreamed things would get to this point.*

That's how young Ralph felt the Saturday evening he sat in a jail cell in the suburban city in which he lived. He felt the shame and humiliation of having to look his father in the eye and admit his failure. It had all started with a lot of little things. He and his friends were just fun-loving teenagers. There was this girl from the church they attended whose family owned a Volkswagen Beetle. It had a set of hubcaps Ralph and his friends just had to have. The girl's house had been quiet all evening, and it was almost midnight. There were no dogs in the immediate neighborhood. The street was an isolated cul-de-sac. Traffic at that hour was practically nonexistent.

He still couldn't figure out how the patrol car just happened to be driving up the street. His friends ran away, escaping through the back yards. But the spotlight from the patrol car landed squarely on him, hubcap in hand, rushing furiously from the driveway where the Beetle sat. He was handcuffed, pushed into the back of the patrol car, then taken to the jail to be booked. Since Ralph was one of the leaders in his church youth group, his humiliation was compounded when his pastor showed up at the jail shortly after his father. As he later put it, "It was one of the most humbling moments of my life. But it made me take a look at myself and the direction my life was headed. It was a crisis, a crossroads for me. And it changed my life forever."

In Mandarin Chinese the word for "crisis" is composed of two characters, one of which means *danger*, the other *opportunity*. Like young Ralph, the New Testament prodigal had reached a crisis point in his life. Things could go either way. Thankfully he made the right choice. Like the process outlined in John 8:32, it was a choice he made based on knowledge of his father's character and the conditions he knew to exist back home. He faced the truth about his own hopeless situation and then chose to move back toward true freedom.

Jesus made His pronouncement about true inner freedom on one of the great religious feast days in Israel. Standing in the temple, He proclaimed Himself to be the light of the world, offering the light of spiritual life to those who followed Him (John 8:12). Immediately, the prominent religious leaders, the scribes and Pharisees, rejected His claim as untrue.

Many others from the crowd that day responded to Him positively. Jesus said to them, "If you abide in My word, you are My disciples indeed."

Start with Knowledge

"And you shall know the truth, and the truth shall make you free," Jesus declared emphatically. Here Jesus identified the first step in finding freedom. It begins with a personal knowledge of God's truth. For those who consider the claims of Christ today, this includes knowing the basic facts about His deity (He is God and man), His perfect, sinless life, His death on the cross to pay for human sin, and His resurrection which guarantees God's promise of eternal life for those who trust in Him.

Though the process begins with these basic facts, it doesn't end there. Instead, it leads to a restructured approach to thinking. The old circuits, the previous patterns, just won't work, any more than files from an IBM computer can be dumped into a Macintosh or vice versa without the appropriate conversion software.

Ultimately, the knowledge of which Jesus spoke is not just a collection of basic facts or even a new mental operating system to process our thinking. Rather, it involves a personal relationship, the kind of personal knowledge that was the passion of another biblical writer, Paul. He wrote, ". . . that I may know Him and the power of His resurrection, and the fellowship of His sufferings, being conformed to His death . . ." (Philippians 3:10). The Greek word Paul used for "know" (*ginosko*) is the same one John records in John 8:32. Earlier in John 8 and again later, Jesus employed another word, *oida*, which is more clearly associated with simply knowing facts. To know the liberating truth, Jesus chose the word which describes knowing with a personal relationship. His point is clear—to know the truth that sets us free means to know Him personally and thereby to have an abundant life (John 10:10).

The young man must have begun to consider the basic facts he knew about his father and his home. His dad was a compassionate man, one who was willing to extend a second chance to those who failed. Furthermore, even the lowliest servant who lived in his dad's household had sufficient food and shelter. Although these facts hadn't been important to the young man when he left home, they must have become an increasingly prominent part of his thinking as his life became more unbearable.

The Greek philosopher Socrates is perhaps best known for urging his students to "know thyself." Modern society has placed a great deal of emphasis on the value of self-knowledge. A contemporary philosopher or psychologist might have suggested that the young prodigal get to know himself better. Such a hypothetical conversation might go like this: "Young man, you need to really know your inner self, to get in touch with your real feelings. Then, you can be a self-actualized, truly fulfilled person."

To which the young man might reply, "I have come to know myself—and I'm cold, hungry, and dirty."

Self-knowledge in itself is a dead end street. Once we get there, we discover we actually know very little. Even though Socrates was right when he suggested that the unexamined life is not worth living, the ultimate goal is not simply to examine ourselves and what we know. What we actually need is to know someone who can make a difference in our condition. For the young prodigal, it was a father who could reach out to him with unconditional love, restore him to his place in the home, and provide for his every need. For us today, it is a loving heavenly Father we can know through faith in His Son, Jesus, who suffered and died to pay for our sins and whose resurrection guarantees that knowing Him personally can make all the difference in the world.

Focus on Truth

The second distinctive in this process of true inner change is that it *focuses on the truth.* That is exactly what began to happen to the young prodigal. He came to realize, as he thought things through, that the hired servants and even the day laborers who showed up to help with the heavy work at harvest time were far better off than he was or could possibly be. It was time for him to quit living his life as though he were following instructions from Joe Isuzu.

"Joe who?" you ask—perhaps you don't remember Joe Isuzu. He was the television pitchman from the 1980s who promised a new automobile costing nine dollars that was supposedly able to get three hundred miles per gallon at speeds of up to one hundred fifty miles per hour. All the time he was making these promises, the words flashed on the television screen below him, "He's lying."

Sadly, telling the truth seems to be pretty much a missing ingredient in our society today. The authors of the book *The Day America Told the Truth* discovered in their research that 91 percent of us in America lie regularly and only 31 percent consider honesty the best policy.[1] Is it any wonder that so many people are trapped by multiple lies and self-deception? Honesty with self had not seemed important to this young prodigal, but at this point he needed to integrate the truth into both his thoughts and actions.

Facing the truth and integrating it into our lives is something we have to deal with in a variety of ways. For example, I may want that new automobile I see on a showroom floor. The truth is I don't have the money to purchase it. I'd like to join my friends on a vacation trip to the beach, but the reality of responsibilities at work demand that I stay home.

A couple of months before the baseball strike of 1994 wiped out the season, several of us had planned to travel to Kansas City for a weekend of ministry, fellowship, and fun. Our Saturday evening schedule called for a visit to one of Kansas City's famous barbecue restaurants, then an evening at Kaufman Stadium watching the Kansas City Royals take on the Cleveland Indians.

It was not until we were actually en route to Kansas City that the truth really hit us—we could take in the barbecue, but there would be no baseball outing. Even though we had formed our plans and purchased our tickets, the baseball players' strike had confronted us with the unpleasant truth that there would be no major league baseball on the Saturday evening in question.

So how can we begin this process of focusing on truth? First, we break through our denial and give up our rationalizations which are basically fancy, emotionally-attractive lies. We stop the projection—the shifting of blame—to parents, siblings, or others. We replace the thought distortions—the "they're out to get me" personalization, the "mountain out of a molehill" magnifications, the "beam in the eye" kind of thinking that refuses to accept responsibility. In short we own our sins, our faults, and our failures.

When we do this, God is thoroughly delighted! God's singular desire is for "truth in the inward parts" (Psalm 51:6). When we've come to admit the truth, we can expect God to provide us with the wisdom we need for right decisions. That's why David wrote in one of the Psalms, "Search me, O God, and know my heart; try me, and know my anxieties; and see if there is any wicked way in me, and lead me in the way everlasting" (Psalm 139:23–24).

One element of this process of securing freedom involves giving up the false beliefs and the fatal concepts to which we have clung tenaciously even though they haven't worked. Beliefs like: somehow I can always run things my own way; I have to perform up to a certain standard to please God or others; I couldn't survive without human approval; or, at some point God will wind up grading everyone on the curve.

Ultimately, giving up on false beliefs comes down to a matter of trust—trusting in Christ for salvation, then trusting in Him for the strength each day to obey Him. Paul summarized it well in one of his letters to first-century believers, "As you therefore have received Christ Jesus the Lord, so walk in Him" (Colossians 2:6).

Whether for salvation or for spiritual life, for direction or for the provision of our needs, securing real freedom ultimately boils down to trust. And delightfully, as we trust Him, we appropriate the power of His Holy Spirit, the One who comes to indwell every believer and who functions as the only true Spirit guide in our age or any age.

There is no other source of liberty—only this truth can set us free.

The young prodigal came to this realization, this moment of truth, because of his hardship. We could say that before this he had been beside himself; after this he came to himself. He recalled the loving protection and care of his father, how he had treated not only his sons but even his servants with fairness and grace. Now the prodigal was ready for that father-son relationship to be restored. His heart and mind had been genuinely changed.

Making a Move Toward Freedom

The third phase of this process involves action. He began the journey back to his father that would lead to real freedom. Freedom was what this young man had wanted in the first place—freedom from his father's oversight, freedom from the restraints and responsibilities of home life, freedom from the mundane uses of the fortune which rightfully belonged to him. In essence, his was the age-old cry of the human soul—of those who once lived in bondage behind the Berlin Wall, those who marched with Martin Luther King Jr., those who braved the guns of Tienamin Square, those who stood against tyranny in the former Soviet Union, and multitudes of others.

When we infuse our minds with the liberating truth of God's Word, it brings life-giving change into our minds and lives. As we act on the truth He has revealed in the Bible, we move decisively toward the kind of freedom that is available nowhere else. But true, ultimate freedom is only found in one place, and that is from the Person who claimed, "I am the Truth" and who backed it up with His perfect life.

How Change Takes Place

The young prodigal's transformation gives us a clue as to how change—genuine and lasting—takes place in people today. It begins with the thought processes. That's why we are so convinced of and committed to the value of teaching the Bible and getting it into people's lives. That's what our ministry at Back to the Bible is all about. We're convinced because we've seen what it has done in our own lives and in the lives of people from every kind of background.

It operates this way. First the thought processes are changed, and then the emotions are touched. Next the will and behavior are affected, and lasting change is effected. Coming to his senses, the young man first thought of the reality of ample food provided even for the day laborers back home. Those individuals had no more work security than the office temps or day laborers of today. Yet here he was, the son—and he was starving to death! The emotion in this assessment of his condition is evident. He perceived a real threat to his life. There was a chance, a good one at that, that he might not survive! But now for the first time, there was a light at the end of the tunnel. A plan began to take shape, and he resolved to carry it out.

At this point we discover the young man engaging in healthy self-talk, purposefully expressing his resolve to carry out the changes in his thinking, "I will arise and go to my father." No more sitting in the corner of the pigpen throwing a pity party for one. It was time to move beyond the wishes, the grief, and the tears. And his father couldn't come riding to his rescue—he had no idea where his son was! Unlike the omniscient heavenly Father, his earthly dad was only human. If there was to be reconciliation and restoration, fellowship and food, then he—the wayward son—would have to take the first step.

Undoubtedly his hunger and the thought of the plentiful food at his father's table was a factor in his decision. Perhaps he also missed his homeland. But as he tired of the constant exposure to pigs and those who owned them, the focus of his thought processes was his father and the relationship he had severed when he abandoned his homestead. He had demanded the inheritance from his father and dishonored him. Now he needed to return to his father and ask for forgiveness. The funds of his inheritance were gone forever. He could never get them back, but maybe in some way he could have his father back.

As he sat in the pigpen, he rehearsed what he would say to his dad. First, there would be a confession. "Father, I have sinned against heaven and before you." Significantly, he chose not to offer excuses or point to extenuating circumstances. He would not blame his older brother, his father, nor any other thing or person. He would simply admit that he had sinned, missed the mark, fallen short of the standard set by God and taught by his father.

Lynette was a beautiful, vivacious teenager who had been active in her youth group, doing well in her studies in a Christian high school, and involved in many extracurricular activities. A personable, outgoing girl, Lynette surrounded herself with friends, one of whom was Jarrod, a young man who attended another school and who had little interest in spiritual things.

Lynette began dating Jarrod exclusively and refused to listen to the advice of parents, teachers, youth pastor, or friends. Before long, the seemingly inevitable thing happened. Lynette was pregnant.

In a tearful conversation with her parents and older sister, Lynette admitted to her prodigal behavior and acknowledged her need to confess her sin to the pastor and elders of her church. Her parents made arrangements for a meeting to take place.

Following the meeting, the pastor and one of the elders stood together on the steps of the church, tears in their eyes, both amazed at what they had heard.

"I can't believe what she said. How incredibly biblical and how mature. She didn't say 'I got pregnant.' Her confession was, 'I was immoral.' "

In similar fashion, this young prodigal acknowledged, "I have sinned against heaven and before you." While it is possible that the phrase "against heaven" could indicate that he considered his sins of such magnitude as to be piled as high as heaven, it seems more likely that he was acknowledging that sin is ultimately against God even more than against those people we violate. For every Jew there was a clear-cut realization from the Old Testament that God extends the loving care of a father (Psalm 103:13). So the son was preparing to return and to confess his sin.

The second component of the plan he rehearsed was that he would simply request employment as a day laborer or even as a household servant rather than acceptance as a returned heir or son. By doing so, he would acknowledge his personal unworthiness and the magnitude of his failure.

It is important to note that since it is a parable, this story does not purport to present every element of the Gospel. Its emphasis is on the significant truth of God's willingness to receive repentant sinners and His joy over their return. The place of Jesus Christ, God's Son, and His death on the cross is amply discussed both elsewhere in Luke and throughout the New Testament.

Yet nothing could be more evident in this parable than the loving invitation of a Father who is eager to extend the forgiveness and freedom He has made available to those who do not deserve to be His children. Like the prodigal, we don't deserve to be children of God. Yet He wants us to be His loving children and His committed disciples. His loving promise to all of us is expressed clearly by Jesus in John 6:37: "All that the Father gives Me will come to Me, and the one who comes to Me I will by no means cast out."

We have seen how the young man began to interact in his mind and heart with the truth about his own hopeless condition and the love and acceptance available at his father's house. It was that truth that set him free, free to make the change of mind that led to the dramatic change in direction his life took. As he took that first step back home, the young man had truly repented.

Start Over

When you've made your plans and they've gone awry,
When you've tried your best 'til there's no more try,
When you've failed yourself and you don't know why
START OVER.

When you've told your friends what you plan to do,
When you've trusted them but they didn't come through,
Now you're all alone and it's up to you
START OVER.

When you think you're finished and want to quit,
When you've bottomed out in life's deepest pit,
When you've tried and tried to get out of it
START OVER.

Starting over means victories won,
Starting over means a race well run,
Starting over means the Lord's "Well done,"
. . . so don't just sit there, START OVER.

—Woodrow Kroll

Endnotes

1.   James Patterson and Peter Kim, *The Day America Told the Truth: What People Really Believe About Everything That Really Matters* (New York: Prentice-Hall, 1991).

CHAPTER FIVE

Welcome Home!

The Prodigal

I face the day again, against the window pane.
I remain your closest friend, and wish you back again.
You wonder how I feel, you think you've pushed too far.
If only you could see this pen scribbling down my heart.
I'll be waiting, I may be young or old and gray, counting the days.
But I'll be waiting, so when I fin'lly see you come
I'll run when I see you, I'll meet you.

But still the days drag on. Why did you decide to go?
Did you only need to see what only time can show?
I'll be waiting, I may be young or old and gray, counting the days.
But I'll be waiting, and when I fin'lly see you come
I'll run when I see you.
I'll be waiting, I may be young or old and gray, counting the days.
But I'll be waiting, and when I fin'lly see you come
I'll run to meet you.

And even if you never do return,
still I will have learned how to love you better.

I'll run to meet you.

And he arose and came to his father. But when he was still a great way off, his father saw him and had compassion, and ran and fell on his neck and kissed him. And the son said to him, "Father, I have sinned against heaven and in your sight, and am no longer worthy to be called your son." But the father said to his servants, "Bring out the best robe and put it on him, and put a ring on his hand and sandals on his feet. And bring the fatted calf here and kill it, and let us eat and be merry; for this my son was dead and is alive again; he was lost and is found." And they began to be merry. (Luke 15:20–24)

This story has inspired everything from Christian music to a Rembrandt masterpiece. It has been the focus of countless sermons and prompted an incalculable number of prodigals to come to faith in Jesus Christ. The scene of the loving father welcoming the returning prodigal is one of the most touching in all of Scripture, not just because of its emotional impact but also for its portrayal of the love and compassion of the father. Here was a father who still loved a son who had deeply wronged him.

As we pointed out earlier, the father is without question the focal point of this parable. Though more is said of the younger son and his journey into the depths of sin and even though the bitter older brother plays a key role, the father who reaches out to both of his sons is the major player in this drama.

We don't know what thoughts went through this father's mind when his son left home, but as fathers ourselves, we can understand the inner agony, intense concern, and even nights of sleepless prayer that must have marked his life while the younger son was away.

Persistent Hope

Of all the father's traits the one that stands out most significantly was his persistent hope. He never gave up the conviction that God would restore his wayward son, that the same young man who had so arrogantly left would one day return home. The text doesn't say this in so many words, but the evidence is there, both in his persistent pattern of watching the nearby road and in the presence of a fattened calf. Even though many wealthy families of that day kept fattened animals for unexpected entertaining, many commentators agree that this one seemed to have a direct connection with the anticipated return of the wayward son.

Then there was Jesus' description of the father spotting the young man in the distance. Though we cannot say so with certainty, the scene Jesus portrayed suggests a father who spent time each day scanning the far stretches of road, hoping for his son's appearance. In essence he was a man of hope, a man whose thinking and life were marked by a determination not to give up even in the face of incredible odds. Perhaps his older son had told him he was wasting his time; maybe his friends or even his hired servants chided him to his face or laughed behind his back. Yet he never gave up hope.

The May 18, 1990, edition of *USA Today* carried a brief obituary of Dorothy Hawkins. This was not unusual in itself, since the paper often selected obituaries of people who had been active in civic affairs in their communities, and Dorothy fit that profile of civic activity. She had been involved in medical research and played a key role in both fund raising and volunteer work at her local library.

But the published obituary failed to include the two most significant facts about the life and death of Dorothy Hawkins. The first was that for years she had been a devout atheist. In fact, according to those who knew her, she was just about as militant as Madelyn Murray O'Hair, to whom she bore a more-than-slight physical resemblance. At her funeral a friend told the minister immediately after the service, "Dorothy warned me forty years ago that I'd have to accept her as an atheist if I intended to be her friend."

The other fact about Dorothy's life, even more remarkable, was that three days prior to her death of colon cancer, she had trusted Christ as Savior in her hospital bed. Her brother and others in her family who were believers had never given up hope that one day she would come to faith.

On Mother's Day, 1990, Dorothy's nephew, whom she had persistently attempted to convert to atheism, explained the Gospel to her one more time. Finally she responded in faith to the Savior from whom she had bitterly wandered as a prodigal for so many years. Humanly speaking, Dorothy never would have made that decision had her brother, Jim, not been the kind of person who, like the father of the prodigal son, never gave up. And according to Jim Hawkins, there is no passage of Scripture he loves better than the story of the prodigal son.

A second important trait of this father was that he genuinely cared for his son. He was a man of compassion. The attitude we see is not that of a father who simply wanted to regain control over a wayward son or to tell him "I told you so." Rather, we see and hear a man motivated by compassion.

Several different words for compassion are found in the New Testament. The one Jesus employed here was usually used for the kind of inward compassion Jesus felt toward the multitudes and toward desperate individuals, such as lepers or the blind. Three times the word is employed in parables—once in Jesus' account of the forgiving master and the indebted servant which deals with the question of forgiveness (Matthew 18:27), once in the account of the Good Samaritan (Luke 10:33), and here of the prodigal's father. In addition to the two parables just mentioned, Luke only uses the word once, to describe Jesus' response to the widow whose only son had died, just before He raised the young man back to life (Luke 7:13). Its distinctive references in the New Testament to Jesus, the Good Samaritan, and to the father of the prodigal show it to signify personal compassion of the highest magnitude.

Authentic Love

The letters and calls we receive in response to our radio ministries indicate that for many people the absence of a loving, caring father is one of the greatest sources of pain in life. Time after time we have heard or read, "My father just didn't care about me. He was indifferent toward us. I never knew that he cared."

Yet here was a father who modeled compassion, a father whose love provided an appropriate parallel to the love of the heavenly Father who gave the supreme sacrifice of His own Son to pay for our sins. This father reached out in love to his son just as God the Father reached out in love to a lost world.

Think of the weeks, the months, perhaps the years he had waited, spending lonely hours each day looking down that road. Sometimes it was empty, at other times filled with caravans and travelers. Whatever the traffic, the father peered intensely into the distance, longing for just one glimpse of his son.

Then one day it happened! His boy was finally coming back—it was his son! Gone were the familiar, comfortable clothes. The young man must have been dirty and disheveled. Perhaps he still smelled like the pigpen where he had been working. But none of this mattered to the father. His son, the son everyone believed was dead, was alive.

His love for this young man, like that of the Lord God for prodigal Israel, was everlasting (Jeremiah 31:3). Certainly it was unconditional, for the son had violated any and every possible condition in a father-son relationship. It was the kind of love extended to us by the Father who "so loved the world that He gave His only begotten Son, that whoever believes in Him should not perish but have everlasting life" (John 3:16). It is the kind of love to which we respond when we trust Jesus Christ as Savior.

Genuine Enthusiasm

His father was not only hopeful and loving, but he was also enthusiastic. We are not told whether his eyes filled with tears or if his heart began to pound with anticipation. But Jesus stated that this father ran to greet his son. It must have struck His listeners as highly unusual since fathers normally didn't do this. We are not told the father's age, but since this was so out of character for Jewish fathers, the verbal picture clearly shows his level of enthusiasm at the return of his prodigal. Driven by his compassion, the father rushed to his son, threw his arms around him—the New Testament uses a descriptive term that literally translated means "he fell on his neck"—and began kissing him. The warmth, the enthusiasm of the embrace, the kisses (it must have truly been a great, big bear hug) no doubt touched the hearts of at least some of those standing around listening to Jesus.

It is traditional in the Middle East to greet someone with an embrace and a kiss on each cheek. But this lengthy, intense hug and shower of kisses certainly demonstrated the joy of this father to have his wayward son back home, the reality of his forgiveness, the intensity of his compassion, and the extent of his affection. Over and over he kissed and embraced his son before the young man had a chance to utter a word of his carefully planned confession. Most of us can probably recall the incredibly enthusiastic greetings, the joyous embraces, and the shower of kisses we've witnessed at the televised release of individuals held hostage by terrorists and of soldiers returning from Operation Desert Storm. That's the kind of enthusiastic greeting this father gave his son. Anyone could see how glad he was to have the boy home.

Bitter-Free Dad

This father also demonstrated a strong degree of forgiveness and self-control plus a remarkable absence of bitterness. He totally refused to utter the four most common words spoken by the parents of prodigals—"I told you so"—and steadfastly avoided such phrases as "Look what you've cost me," "I guess you know how difficult these days have been for all of us here," or "Do you realize the agony you've put me through?" None of that mattered now—the son he loved had come home.

The father's response remarkably parallels the compassion of our heavenly Father. As the prophet Isaiah so clearly pointed out centuries before, "All we like sheep have gone astray; we have turned, everyone, to his own ways; and the Lord has laid on Him the iniquity of us all."

Clearly we have all become estranged from God, like prodigals, turning our back on the heavenly Father to go our chosen ways. But the Lord laid on Jesus our iniquity—all the sins we ever committed. And when we come to Him, He welcomes us with affection and forgiveness. He forgives our sin, provides for our every need, and delights in the prospect of spending eternity with us.

But what about rebuke? you ask. Why didn't this father verbally chastise this wayward son? Didn't he have a right to? Many centuries before Christ, the wise King Solomon wrote, "To everything there is a season, a time for every purpose under heaven" (Ecclesiastes 3:1). Certainly there is a time for loving rebuke. In the New Testament the apostle Paul encouraged believers to "warn those who are unruly" (1 Thessalonians 5:14). Yet in the same breath he urged them to "comfort the fainthearted, uphold the weak, be patient with all" (vv. 14b–15). Without question there is time for rebuke, for a loving confrontation, particularly when we are in contact with an unrepentant prodigal. But to rebuke or censure this son under these circumstances would have been unthinkable. He had headed home repentant, to ask for forgiveness. In fact, the very first words out of his mouth were, "Father, I have sinned against heaven and before you."

Perhaps they are the most difficult words in any language—"I have sinned." But following his plan, the young man spoke them. Significantly, he first acknowledged that his sin was against God, then against his father. Ultimately, every sin we commit is an affront to our loving heavenly Father and our gracious Savior.

Like his loving heavenly counterpart, this earthly father immediately chose to forgive without having to consider or debate the issue in his mind. Our heavenly Father forgives because He has lovingly provided for our salvation through the death of His Son. This earthly father was eager to provide for every need of his famished, exhausted, discouraged young son.

The total absence of bitterness on the part of this father is remarkable because bitterness is one of the most common and difficult spiritual problems. As the Bible points out, a root of bitterness can often grow out of adverse circumstances, affecting us and those around us (Hebrews 12:15). Bitterness can pollute family relationships (Colossians 3:19) and bring about the dissolution of even the strongest ties. The younger son had exhibited signs of bitterness when he demanded his inheritance and angrily left home. In the chapter to follow, we will see how the young man's older brother bitterly greeted his return. Yet this father, who humanly had every right to feel bitter, was admirably bitter-free.

Prolonged Anger

What is bitterness anyway? First, bitterness always involves anger. The clear link between the two was established by the apostle Paul when he wrote, "'Be angry, and do not sin': do not let the sun go down on your wrath. . . . Let all bitterness, wrath, anger, clamor and evil speaking be put away from you, with all malice. And be kind to one another, tender-hearted, forgiving one another, as God in Christ forgave you" (Ephesians 4:26, 31–32). To prolong anger will cause us to become bitter. Bitterness must be decisively put away by those who would walk by the Spirit in fellowship with God (Ephesians 4:31). Bitterness is frequently associated with jealousy (Acts 8:23) and may develop from adversity, including God's discipline (Hebrews 12:15). It is a frequent outgrowth of inner personal strife and conflict (James 3:14).

The connection between a bitter attitude and corrupt, negative conversation is underscored by the Bible in James 3:11 as well as Ephesians 4:29 and 31. The significance of this link can be seen in the life of the elder brother whose bitter attitude toward both his father and his younger brother was expressed in his harsh words with his father.

As we examine the topic of bitterness throughout Scripture, we come to the conclusion that there are three major components. The first, as we have noted, is anger. Certainly this father, humanly speaking, had every right to be angry with his son. After all, the young upstart had spat in the face of everything his father stood for, causing his dad no end of grief and humiliation.

Anger itself, however, is not always a sinful emotion. Jesus exhibited anger several times in his life, most notably when He forced merchants out of the temple grounds and on occasions when He confronted the arrogant unbelief of the Pharisees. So, how should we handle anger appropriately and fulfill the Bible's mandate to "be angry, and do not sin?" By resolving it prior to bedtime or, as the Bible says, "Do not let the sun go down on your wrath."

This statement identifies the second major element in bitterness. It involves not simply anger, but prolonged anger. Sadly, many believers refuse to handle anger biblically. Instead they stuff it away, trying to pretend it doesn't exist. Often they are unaware of a subtle, definite urge to get revenge rather than extend the kind of forgiveness God in Christ extended to us. Three times in the New Testament we are urged not to take vengeance:

"Repay no one evil for evil. . . . Beloved, do not avenge yourselves, but rather give place to wrath; for it is written, 'Vengeance is Mine, I will repay,' says the Lord. 'Therefore if your enemy hungers, feed him; if he thirsts, give him a drink; for in so doing you will heap coals of fire on his head '" (Romans 12:17, 19–20).

"See that no one renders evil for evil to anyone, but always pursue what is good, both for yourselves and for all" (1 Thessalonians 5:15).

"Finally, all of you be of one mind, having compassion for one another; love as brothers, be tenderhearted, be courteous; not returning evil for evil or reviling for reviling, but on the contrary blessing, knowing that you were called to this, that you may inherit a blessing" (1 Peter 3:8–9).

This is precisely the response exhibited by the father who, joyful and excited, extended the official Old Testament "blessing," which included meaningful touch and a positive future, to the young vagabond who had finally returned.[1] Such incredible, loving forgiveness wasn't what the prodigal expected or what he deserved. It was far more! In like manner the amazing, gracious response of our loving, forgiving heavenly Father is far more than we would expect or ever deserve.

All He Was Looking For

This prodigal son had left home looking for freedom. He had hoped to find people who really appreciated him. Instead he found himself, as an Old Testament author wrote centuries earlier, simply "chasing after the wind," discovering only emptiness and frustration of spirit.

But when the young man returned home where he belonged, he found everything he had been looking for. And it had been there all the time. He had just been too blind to see it. Notice the incredible honor which the father extended to him. The son had put it so clearly, "I am no longer worthy to be called your son." Brushing aside that admission, the father issued a chain of instruction to his servants, all designed to honor his son. He had come home, but the calculated proposal designed to get the only thing he thought he was worthy to receive was ignored. Instead the father in joyful, spontaneous love gave him all the boy's heart had ever wanted and much more.

First came the robe of honor. This stately, ceremonial robe, which stretched all the way to the feet, colorful and finely woven of the highest quality fabric, was quite similar to the multicolored robe the Old Testament patriarch Jacob gave his favorite son, Joseph. That robe signified that Joseph was the honored son, chosen by his father to be the heir. Without question, it represented an incredible honor bestowed on this former prodigal.

In quick succession, still more evidences of honor were presented. Next was a ring of beauty and quality. In first-century culture such a ring was a symbol of authority. Business transactions were sealed when a signet ring was pressed into wax. By giving this ring, the father indicated that his son now had the privilege of exercising the authority of the father and conducting his business.

Next came the sandals—servants never wore them, only free men. We don't know what had happened to the shoes in which the young man had left home. Perhaps they had worn out, been sold for food, or been ruined working in the pigpen. What had happened to them wasn't the issue. The father wouldn't allow his son to be seen barefoot by anyone. It was important to get sandals on his son's feet quickly so that everyone would realize he was being received back not as a servant but as a son. How remarkable that the one who just wanted to come home as a day laborer was now honored as a fully equal member of the family!

Beyond all this the father commanded the servants to fetch the fattened calf and prepare it. Certainly such a joyful occasion demanded a celebration. The banquet described by Jesus clued his listeners in to the significance of this parable. This wayward son had now become the guest of honor at a feast. The listeners didn't miss the ultimate significance of such a banquet since the Old Testament prophets used such language to describe the coming kingdom of God. What a radical thought, that God would welcome prodigal sinners and honor them in His kingdom! It was a jolting thought to many, but one they couldn't miss.

The honor bestowed by this father, the great joy with which he lavished the gifts, the spontaneous magnitude of the feast he ordered—all demonstrated how clearly and completely he had forgiven and welcomed back his wayward son. The father's simple yet profound statement summarized the true significance of the occasion—"For this my son was dead and is alive again; he was lost and is found."

Jesus drove home the point of His parable with vivid clarity—the Father in heaven actively reaches out to the lost and rejoices when they return. He clearly wants to extend forgiveness and life to those who are spiritually dead. Those who were open to His message couldn't miss His point. The past could be wiped away, offenses forgiven, and sin removed from the books. Everything the young man had done to his father and everything he had done after he left home was forgiven in full. In the same way the Father in heaven wishes to forgive all our sins and failures.

What a remarkable picture of the love and forgiveness extended by the heavenly Father to all who have tried to go their own way like the prodigal! How tragic that so many of the people who needed it the most remained untouched by Jesus' message of loving forgiveness.

Lesson From a Prodigal

There's a lesson to learn from the prodigal son:
We haven't been put here to be Number One.
Our gracious Lord has in mercy decreed
That we love one another and not live for greed.

When we turn from this mandate, start living for self,
We're likely to find ourselves put on the shelf.
Driven by pleasure, a life on the go;
Learning the hard way, we reap what we sow.

Yet like the prodigal we can return
To the Father in heaven, whose mercy we spurned;
Restored to His fellowship, gripped by His love,
We can model to others His life from above.

—Juanita Hawkins

Endnotes

1.   For a full discussion of the concept of the blessing, see *The Gift of the Blessing* by Gary Smalley and John Trent (Nashville: Thomas Nelson, 1993).

CHAPTER SIX

Big Brother

Forgive Us Our Sins As We Forgive

How can Your pardon reach and bless
    the unforgiving heart
That broods on wrongs and will not let
    old bitterness depart?

In blazing light Your cross reveals
    the truth we dimly know;
How small the debts men owe to us;
    how great our debt to You.

Lord, cleanse the depths within our souls,
    and bid resentment cease;
Then reconciled to God and man,
    our lives will spread Your peace.

—Rosamond E. Herklots

Now his older son was in the field. And as he came and drew near to the house, he heard music and dancing. So he called one of the servants and asked what these things meant. And he said to him, "Your brother has come, and because he has received him safe and sound, your father has killed the fatted calf." But he was angry and would not go in. Therefore his father came out and pleaded with him. So he answered and said to his father, "Lo, these many years I have been serving you; I never transgressed your commandment at any time; and yet you never gave me a young goat, that I might make merry with my friends. But as soon as this son of yours came, who has devoured your livelihood with harlots, you killed the fatted calf for him." (Luke 15:25–30)

When Paul "Bear" Bryant established his record at the University of Alabama as the winningest college football coach ever, he was fond of telling sports writers and reporters that every football game turned on a few key plays. For any team on any given Saturday, winning or losing boiled down to being prepared for those plays and making the right decisions when they happened.

There's a parallel to this axiom in the lives of individuals and families. Making the right decision at a critical point can ensure health, success, and well-being—physically, materially, and spiritually. The wrong choice can lead to personal disaster, family conflict, and ultimate ruin.

The day the younger son demanded his inheritance certainly precipitated such a crisis point for the three members of his family. When he left, the prodigal began moving inexorably down the road to ruin. On the other hand his father, who could have given up or acted hastily, instead exercised the kind of long-suffering steadfastness he should have as a parent.

The Family Hero

And the older brother? No question about it—he could have chosen to leave just like his brother. Or he could have followed the other fork in the road, opted to remain home, do his job, and take care of his father just as any dutiful older son was supposed to do. And that's exactly what he decided to do. Stay home, work hard, exercise responsibility. Whenever his father needed anything, he could always count on his eldest son to be there for him.

Had this family been a case study from modern psychology, the younger son might have been labeled the "scapegoat," the one who rebels against the family and winds up getting into serious problems. On the other hand, the oldest son seemed to perfectly fit the role of "family hero." He had probably done well in his studies at the synagogue, conscientiously carried out the tasks his father gave him to do, and worked well with the servants and others in the community.

As there are in all communities, there were gossips then as well, except they probably had only good things to say about the older brother.

"He's going to be a real pillar in the community."

"It's a shame the way his younger brother has disgraced the family."

"He's the kind of son any father would want. His father must be really proud of him. He's always there to help his dad, and he's so dedicated in following the religious teaching of our people. What a great catch for some lucky girl!"

During that initial crisis, it appeared that this older brother made the right choice, and outwardly he did. Yet on the inside he apparently made a decision that resulted in the wrong choice at the next crisis point he faced. It was a choice that had the potential to be just as devastating as that of his younger brother. The elder son chose to harbor bitterness and resentment toward the two most important people in his life. While outwardly he appeared to be a hero, on the inside he was just another angry, resentful person, trying to keep those feelings hidden from the people around him.

So while the father evidenced none of the dysfunction seen in so many modern-day fathers, both sons were clearly dysfunctional. Since every member of the human race has been affected by sin, even children of parents who do well can exhibit signs of dysfunction. The older brother did a pretty good job of it for a while. But then, out of the blue, the brother he resented so deeply and felt so superior to decided to come home.

Rembrandt's painting of the return of the prodigal contains at least one detail in which he has taken what might be termed artistic license with the account of Scripture. Jesus' sequence of events has the older brother out in the field when the younger son returned and the celebration began.

The brother was probably not around the house to welcome his brother due to his conscientious, responsible way of approaching his personal duties. That's the most obvious explanation, and it seems there's an element of truth to it.

However, we suspect there is another factor as well. It is suggested by the attitude the brother displayed when he found out about the party his father was throwing and heard why. We suspect his absence from this scene demonstrated a distance in his relationship not only with his brother but with his father as well. It seems this son had neither inherited nor learned the people skills or the ability to encourage which were the hallmarks of his father.

How easy it is to lose sight of what is really important while becoming wrapped up in the mechanics of fulfilling day-to-day responsibilities. Recently we heard the story of the owner of a large grocery store who had become obsessed with catching shoplifters. This man had installed several thousand dollars' worth of surveillance cameras, monitors, and other detection equipment. Instead of devoting attention to the overall management of his supermarket, this man wound up spending hours in the surveillance room trying to catch shoplifters. As a result, his business declined. He failed to see, however, that his obsession with a small part of the larger operation was destroying the business itself.

In a similar situation, we also heard of a youth pastor of whom his senior pastor said, "He was far more concerned about making sure the door was locked at the church building and the premises kept clean than over whether anything significant was happening in the lives of the teenagers to whom he ministered."

Both the supermarket owner and the youth pastor had failed to see the forest for the trees. Similarly, the older brother's narrow focus on responsibilities caused him to miss the higher priority of relationships.

This young man had been outwardly obedient to the commands of the Old Testament law. Yet he kept those laws the same way the Pharisees did, giving careful attention to external appearances—the letter of the law—while repudiating the inner dimension, the spirit of the law.

At this point in His ministry, Jesus began to teach the multitudes that all the Law could be summed in the word *love*—a wholehearted love for God plus an unconditional love for people (Luke 10:26–28). It was evident that the religious group called the Pharisees were greatly lacking in that essential ingredient of love. The same could be said of this older brother. His raging response to the father's explanation demonstrated that deep inside he had despised his younger brother all along. Perhaps he nursed his inner bitterness with thoughts of how he would handle the confrontation if he ever ran into the irresponsible bum again. He'd certainly let him know what a sorry excuse for a son and a brother he had been. But then he thought with smug satisfaction that his brother would probably never return—and if he ever did, it would still be too soon! So his inner anger must have simmered day after day, month after month, perhaps year after year. Sooner or later it was bound to come to a boil and explode in a hateful outburst.

He undoubtedly felt self-righteously indignant toward the younger brother who was clearly a prodigal. Outwardly, the older brother appeared to be the ideal son just as the younger son appeared to be a prodigal. But the older boy was also a prodigal—in heart. What a remarkable irony! While the younger brother's hands had been feeding carob pods to the pigs far away, his heart had shifted back home. At the same time, while the older brother's hands were busy serving in his father's fields, his heart wasn't really in his home or family.

Sounds of a Party

When He told the story of the prodigal, Jesus didn't give the time sequence. Perhaps the older brother came in from the field for lunch, or maybe he had finished the day's chores and was headed in to relax, have dinner, and plan the next day's work. Whatever was on his mind as he approached the house, he heard the sounds of a party, music, and dancing. Had he lived today, he might have consulted his Daytimer or pocket planner, scratched his head, and said, "That's funny, we didn't have any social occasion on the calendar for tonight. I wonder if there was something planned that Dad forgot to tell me about." It's also possible he actually suspected that his brother had returned, and that certainly wouldn't make him happy. In any case, the festive sounds of music from entertainers the father may have hired for the occasion told him this must be an important celebration.

Whatever his thoughts, he encountered one of the household servants—the term Jesus used here was different from the word for the day laborers or slaves that the young prodigal used in verse 17. The servant's reply must have felt like a red-hot iron driven into the older brother's heart, "Your brother has come, and because he has received him safe and sound, your father has killed the fatted calf."

In one sense, the return of the prodigal was not a surprise to the father. The wording of the text implies that he would actually leave his home and go to a spot from which he could observe the caravan route and travelers and watch for the arrival of his son. Undoubtedly he had prayed each day for the young boy's return, perhaps in family prayers. In all likelihood the older brother had gritted his teeth whenever his dad would pray for the young man's return. Perhaps he would even voice a prayer to counter his dad's!

This older brother certainly bore no resemblance to either of the main characters in the two earlier components of Jesus' extended parable—the shepherd who sought his wandering sheep or the housewife who searched for her missing coin. Like the father, they had both searched diligently for what was missing, expecting to find it. And like the father, they rejoiced intensely when they found the lost item. They were exultant—just like the angels in heaven who rejoice when a sinner repents. But not this older brother.

If you had asked him, he might have told you, "That brother of mine is just no good, pure and simple. He showed no respect for our father, for the family, for his responsibilities, or even for God. He squandered his inheritance on prostitutes. There's no other way to describe him but as a low-down sinner."

In reality, this older brother was also a sinner and a prodigal at heart. He had demonstrated a shameful lack of concern for his lost brother and a sinful lack of faith in God's ability to bring him home. In addition, the anger he felt when he heard his brother had returned and the rage he vented on his father revealed a long-simmering bitterness under his self-righteous facade.

Bitter Brother

As we suggested earlier, bitterness is one of the most serious emotional and spiritual problems a person can have. When the apostle Paul addressed the problem of unhealthy communication in relationships, he urged, "'Be angry and do not sin'; do not let the sun go down on your wrath" (Ephesians 4:26). In this carefully worded statement, Paul pinpoints the essential nature of bitterness as anger prolonged beyond the time when it should be resolved. First-century custom dictated that people went to bed when the sun went down; thus Paul's point is that we need to recognize feelings of unresolved anger and deal with them on the same day.

Therefore, it is bitterness—the unhealthy failure to resolve anger coupled with the cultivation of a subtle yet definite desire to get even— that is wrong. Twice in his letters Paul warned that revenge must be left to God (Romans 12:19; 1 Thessalonians 5:15). It seems likely that it was such bitter feelings that led to the outburst of anger on the part of this older brother.

For the older brother there was no joy and none of the forgiveness exhibited by the father who had been far more deeply and directly hurt by the actions of the prodigal son. The dialogue between the father and his eldest son confirms that this was a selfish anger, an anger that went beyond what is reasonable and right and an anger that grew out of extended bitterness.

The bitter anger on the part of this brother is inextricably bound up in the purpose of the story. As we observed before, among Jesus' listeners were a group of people who not only were filled with a snobbish arrogance and a self-righteousness that caused them to see no spiritual need on their own part, but they had also exhibited a bitter hostility and intense anger toward Jesus because of His warm acceptance of those who were sinners. Thus, the bitter rejection by the older brother of his father's gracious attitude toward a sinful prodigal parallels the bitterness the Pharisees had shown toward Jesus because of His compassion for tax collectors and other sinners.

The obvious question that comes to mind is how could a young man with such promise and potential, who chose to do the right thing, become so consumed by this kind of bitterness? More to the point, how can we avoid falling into the same bitter trap in our lives?

Although the Greek word translated "bitter" in the New Testament isn't used here, other uses of the word throughout the New Testament provide significant insight into the spiritual problem that infected this older brother and the common causes of bitterness. In one instance, bitterness grew from intense jealousy (Acts 8:23). It is identified as one of a host of problems that is characteristic of fallen humanity (Romans 3:14). It can grow from a harsh lack of love (Colossians 3:19), from uncontrolled, prolonged anger mixed with an unforgiving spirit (Ephesians 4:31), from a component of interpersonal conflict or strife (James 3:14), and as a result of one's failure to respond appropriately to difficulty (Hebrews 12:15). These same factors can generate bitterness in relationships today, bitterness toward spouses, bitterness toward parents or children, even bitterness toward God.

Celia had been the female counterpart to the older brother in her family. While her younger sister did poorly in school, then finally quit to begin living with a young man, Celia was always careful to do well in school, be faithful in church attendance, and otherwise be the dutiful daughter her parents expected. She never married, preferring to say, "God has called me to serve Him and take care of my parents."

But what seemed like a sweet disposition on Celia's part erupted into rage shortly after her sister broke off the relationship with the young man she had been living with, yielded her life to the Lord, and became engaged to a young man who was active in their local church.

"I can't believe my parents would be taken in by that phony," she retorted sarcastically to a friend from church who asked if she was excited about being in her sister's wedding. "I don't think there will be a wedding. I don't think there should be a wedding. She has not respected my parents and has drained them of money they didn't have to support her ungodly lifestyle." Sure enough Celia refused to participate in her sister's wedding. She attended, however, at the request of her parents. And as one neutral observer expressed it, "You could cut the tension with a knife."

How important it is that each of us examines his or her own heart and roots out any semblance of bitterness. Like common weeds that if left unchecked will choke out the carefully planted grass of a lawn, feelings of bitterness can bring quick and devastating ruin to our spiritual lives. Bitter feelings serve as a major deterrent to fellowship with our heavenly Father as well as with our brothers and sisters in Christ.

That's exactly what happened to this older brother. How his angry refusal to join the celebration must have hurt his father! The occasion clearly called for rejoicing. Yet the young man chose to be bitter. He was bitter at his father because he took his brother back into the family, bitter because he threw a party to welcome the repentant prodigal, and bitter toward the brother for upsetting the equilibrium of his own comfortable lifestyle. It's not hard to imagine the message he might have given the servant to relay to his father. "I have absolutely no intention of coming in for a party—not as long as that brother is there. It's either him or me!"

A Father's Love

Both of these brothers were blessed with a remarkable father, a father Jesus had already described as filled with compassion (Luke 15:20). The abundant, paternal compassion that had been showered on the wayward son was now extended to the bitter, hypocritical son who refused to grace the party his father had given.

The father could have thrown up his hands in exasperation and said, "I never can get these boys to cooperate. If it's not one, it's the other!" Certainly any of us might have been tempted to do so. But this Jewish father is a model of the response of a heavenly Father who cares about both publicans and Pharisees. Instead of waiting inside or sending a message back by one of the servants, he left the celebration and went out to the older brother. He showed no favoritism nor did he scold or deliver a sermon. Instead, he sought to encourage a right response from his older son.

Part of this father's encouragement involved a willingness to listen as the older son who had been with him all along poured out his pent-up rage. Just as in the case of many teenagers and young adults today, beneath that rage was intense pain and deep hurt. The pain was evident in the words with which he lashed out at his father, the charges he leveled, and the intense emotion he expressed.

"Look! All these years I've slaved for you. Never disobeyed your orders! But you never gave me even a young goat so I could party with my friends—much less a fattened calf. But the minute this 'son' of yours, who wasted your wealth with prostitutes—the minute he shows up, you kill the fatted calf for him?"

What a tribute to this father that he stood there, listened to the diatribe of his son, and allowed him to get the emotion out of his system.

Walt's son Ed had decided to move out on his own following graduation from high school. For several months he tried to make ends meet, struggling through his first year of college and a succession of low-paying jobs.

Finally, in frustration, Ed called his parents and asked if he could move back home. Walt and Susan were more than agreeable.

Shortly after returning to his parents' home, Ed asked if he could assist Walt in his construction work. Without hesitation Walt agreed.

As the two men left for work the first day, Walt sensed something was bothering Ed. When he asked, a mixture of feelings came pouring out. "I feel like I've fouled up things for you and Mom, not just for me. I've been a real pain, and I know it. I don't even feel like it's fair of you to offer me work—and I'm really upset at some of my friends who stole my stereo and the camera I had borrowed from you and Mom."

Patiently listening to his son's emotional confession, Walt reassured his son of both parents' love and acceptance. When Ed apologized for being so upset, Walt replied, "Don't feel badly about that, son. That's what we're here for. It's healthy to share our feelings with each other. You've been through a lot. I'm glad you feel free to share your hurt and frustration with me. I want you to feel free to do so any time."

The point, as we can also see from the father's response to the older brother, is that one of the most effective ways to encourage someone is to listen and in the process draw out the emotion of the heart.

Feelings of Distance

There may have been an element of truth in the accusation of this angry older brother. Perhaps the father had taken his older son for granted. Maybe he had never thought to provide a special treat or a celebration. There could have been some emotional distance as there often is between fathers and sons now.

It's important to remember that Jesus' account is given in the form of a parable, a method of teaching a specific truth. While the father represents the heavenly Father in his joy, forgiveness, and patience toward both sons, Jesus isn't trying to tell us he was a perfect human father. We don't know what his imperfections were, yet we can learn from the accusations of the elder brother certain things that we fathers need to avoid in our relationships—such as allowing emotional distance to develop, taking our children for granted, or giving out responsibility without providing special times of reward.

While the major focus of his anger was toward his brother, the pain was more intense because this brother felt that his father didn't appreciate him. He felt like he had never been given a pat on the back, never heard a thank you or an expression of love. The intensity of the older brother's reaction to his father over what he perceived as preferential treatment for one who deserved the opposite caused him to sarcastically refer to his brother as "your son." Without question, this father did love both his sons. He certainly must have appreciated the responsibility and service of his firstborn. Yet, in all likelihood, he had just not been able to verbalize his feelings.

Furthermore, although his charge that his brother "squandered his inheritance with prostitutes" may have been accurate, this brother apparently had no way of knowing for sure. He hadn't taken the time to seek out his brother, confront him over his misbehavior, and lovingly do what an older brother should have done for one who has strayed from the straight and narrow. Instead, his attitude may have actually masked the lust in his own heart. Perhaps beneath his self-righteous facade lurked the dark realization that had he followed the path of his brother, that's how he would have wasted the estate.

Like many individuals today, this older brother had probably established a hierarchy of sins in his thinking. Sins like blowing one's inheritance or visiting a prostitute probably ranked first and second on his list of the top ten sins anyone could commit; yet he probably didn't even see that he could be guilty of sins like bitterness, inappropriate anger, jealousy, or stubborn unbelief. No, the splinter in his brother's eye and even the speck in his father's were clearly visible to him. The massive beam in his own eye, however, kept him from seeing the truth that could set him free.

And that's where the story of this older brother ends. For years he refused to deal with his resentment. Then, at a critical crisis point in his life, he allowed it to boil over in an outburst of rage that alienated him from his father and his family. Jesus didn't tell his listeners any more about how this older brother responded. He left him with the call to leave his bitterness, to respond in loving forgiveness to his father's invitation.

Perhaps as you've read this chapter, you have sensed in some ways a kinship with the older brother. Resentment has been present in your life, perhaps building up over the years. You've never honestly confronted your brother, sister, father, or your child, your friend, neighbor, or colleague at work. As a result the bitterness has kept growing like an unseen cancer, getting harder and harder to conceal.

Perhaps it erupted one day in fifty dollars worth of rage over fifty cents worth of wrong. Harsh words were spoken, words that couldn't be retracted. Venomous emotion was allowed to poison what had previously been a loving relationship.

Can anything be done?

God's loving answer is, Yes. The heavenly Father's invitation is still open. While there is life, while there is opportunity, go to your brother, sister, father, or child. Be reconciled. Take that step. Don't be like the self-righteous older brother, allowing bitter feelings of resentment to ruin the joys of life for you and others.

Every day, every situation brings the new choice—bitter or better?

CHAPTER SEVEN

Reconciled to His Father

Bring Him Home

God on high, hear my prayer.
In my need You have always been there.
He is young, he is afraid. Let him rest, heaven-blessed.
Bring him home. Bring him home. Bring him home.

Bring him peace, bring him joy. He is young. He is only a boy.
You can take, you can give. Let him be, let him live.
If I die, let me bring him home.

"Bring Him Home," from the Musicale "Les Misérables" by Alain Boublil and Claude-Michel Schönberg. Lyrics by Alain Boublil and Herbert Kretzmer. Music by Claude-Michel Schönberg. © Alain Boublil Music Ltd. (ASCAP). Used by permission.

*And he said to him, "Son, you are always with me, and all that I
have is yours. It was right that we should make merry and be glad, for
your brother was dead and is alive again, and was lost and is found."*
(Luke 15:31–32)

Ben Franklin included in his popular almanac the old saying, "One
man's meat is another man's poison." Certainly the crisis that
precipitates one person's miserable failure often provides the
opportunity for another's distinctive and unique success.

Neville Chamberlain was prime minister of Great Britain when
that country declared war against Nazi Germany on September 3,
1939. The war effort was going poorly. On April 9, 1940, Germany
launched an attack against Norway. The Five-Pronged Attack, as it
was labeled, under the direction of German grand admiral Erich Raeder,
quickly put Norway in German hands and left Britain even more
concerned than ever since now Hitler had gained both naval and air
bases from which to operate against Great Britain.[1]

Chamberlain had been convinced that only an economic blockade
was needed as a major weapon against Germany. But the failure in
Norway left the British people less convinced than ever of his ability
to lead the nation during wartime. Within a month Parliament
demanded that Chamberlain resign. His resignation on May 10, 1940,
opened the door for the appointment of the man who had served him
as first lord of the Admiralty, Winston Churchill. Three days after
being appointed prime minister, Churchill told the House of Commons,
"I have nothing to offer but blood, toil, tears and sweat." But he
promised victory, however long and hard the road might be. Over and
over again his leadership and his words of encouragement inspired the
nation, and when the war in Europe ended, Churchill received the
accolades he so richly deserved.

In similar fashion, what turned out to be a crisis of failure for the
older brother became a crowning moment for the loving father. He
became living proof of the proverb spoken by a wise father centuries
earlier, "He who heeds the word wisely will find good, and whoever
trusts in the LORD, happy is he" (Proverbs 16:20).

Wise and Fair

The wisdom with which this father handled a delicate situation can
be seen in the fair way he treated both sons. Filled with compassion,
he reached out to each one. Each had given him occasion to become
exasperated or express anger. Instead, he exercised loving self-control.

After listening to the intense emotion the older son unloaded on him, he responded carefully and wisely.

Addressing him directly as "Son," he reminded him of his continued commitment both to him as a son and to his rightful inheritance as the firstborn. Overlooking the disrespect expressed by his son's use of the word "look," he responded with gracious respect and genuine tenderness. Nothing had changed in the relationship between the father and his oldest, and he made that fact clear in both his words and his tone of speech.

Undoubtedly, the father had been deeply hurt by both his boys. Neither seemed to really love him, nor care for the other. Yet this father, as he spoke first to the wayward son, then to the one who had remained home, seemed intent on producing a reconciliation. He sought to do so by reminding this older brother of his continued and important role in the household.

However, the most important message the father gave the older son, and the climactic point of Jesus' parable, is the statement this father makes in verse 32. His comments do not come from personal weakness or vacillation but out of genuine loving strength.

"We had to celebrate. No question about it. To celebrate and be glad was demanded by the circumstances."

Gently yet pointedly the father rebuked the older brother's reference to his sibling as "your son." The father explained the basic reason for the celebration. "This brother of yours was dead, and is alive again! He was lost and is found!"

The Truth of Reconciliation

This incredible account of a loving father who became reconciled with his wayward son and who sought to bring together the two brothers beautifully exemplifies two key aspects of the marvelous truth of reconciliation spelled out in one of Paul's letter to first-century Christians.

In the second chapter of Ephesians, Paul writes that we all were "dead" in our sinfulness, living under Satan's dominion, walking according to the world's way of thinking and doing, and dominated by the desires of the selfish inner person (vv. 1–4). In a crucial transition, he employs the two words which ultimately make the greatest difference: "But God . . ."

Like the father in the account of the prodigal, God is the One who ultimately makes the difference, who first of all provides the personal reconciliation we desperately need to be right with Him. He made this reconciliation possible by giving us life in Jesus Christ and a heavenly position based on salvation by His grace (vv. 5–10). Like the prodigal son who had been dead and was alive because of his father's gracious and loving response, we who were dead are now alive through the heavenly Father.

Furthermore, Paul describes God the Father as the engineer of the interpersonal dimension of reconciliation which is perhaps best exemplified by the centuries-long conflict between Jew and Gentile that flourished in Paul's time. Through Jesus's death for human sin, the chronic enmity between Jews and Gentiles was removed. Those who were at odds with each other about spiritual issues could now be reconciled to each other (v. 15) as well as to God (v. 16).

Trust Him Now

There are two practical implications to this incredible teaching. First, for those who have never trusted Christ as Savior, there simply is no other way. We cannot make ourselves right with God. We have no other recourse. As Billy Graham so clearly explained when he conducted the funeral of former President Richard Nixon, there is but one way to be rightly related to God, and that is through Jesus Christ.

If you have been reading about the prodigal to this point and have not yet confessed your own sinfulness, acknowledged your need of a Savior, and placed your trust in Him, there is no better time than now. Why not simply bow your head at this moment and acknowledge that Jesus Christ, God's Son, died on the cross to reconcile you to God and rose again from the dead to guarantee the effectiveness of that reconciliation. Simply express to the Lord that you are trusting in Christ and Christ alone as your only way to be right with the heavenly Father. Then thank Him for forgiving you and giving you new spiritual life.

The second implication of this great truth of reconciliation is how God can reconcile families, churches, and others when the inevitable conflicts of life occur. While the Christian ideal is for believers to be united in spirit and joined in peace (Ephesians 4:3), the practical reality of life in a fallen world is that conflicts and relational fractures are likely to occur.

Philip, Charles, and Mandy had always been close siblings, beginning with their growing-up years and continuing after all three had married and established their own homes. They took vacations together, attended church together, and watched their kids play soccer and Little League baseball.

Then, when their parents were killed in an automobile accident, an even greater tragedy occurred. The reading of the will and the division of the parents' estate created a rift among all three siblings. Philip and Charles had been in business together—that relationship ended bitterly, and for several years the three families had nothing to do with each other. One family changed churches. Another dropped out of church altogether.

Then during a routine physical checkup, Mandy discovered she had breast cancer. At first, she and her husband decided not to tell her two brothers and their families. After all, there was little more than Christmas card communication. But as Mandy and her husband, Hal, talked with their pastor, they both became convinced that perhaps God could use this experience as a catalyst for bringing about reconciliation in the family. That's exactly what happened when the three couples got together. It wasn't an easy time—long-buried feelings had to be examined, forgiveness extended and intense feelings processed and released. Yet that initial meeting led to a complete restoration of fellowship among the three couples and a strengthening of spiritual life in each home. As Charles's wife, Linda, put it later, "We finally realized life was too short to bear grudges against each other. We're not only family, but we're part of God's family, too."

Overcoming Barriers

This same principle can work effectively in divisions and splits within local churches, in conflicts at work, and can even lead to the resolution of racially-based conflict. The principle is that if the greater is true, the lesser is true. If God could reconcile us, who at heart were His enemies, by the death of His Son, then He can bring about reconciliation in any human relationship.

Once there were two brothers who each received a bicycle for Christmas. A short time later the two brothers began quarreling. Afterward, one angrily cut all the spokes out of the wheels on his brother's bicycle. When the other saw what his brother had done to his bicycle, he responded by cutting the spokes from his brother's bike.

So who was hurt the worst? The younger brother? The older brother? Neither—it was the father. Not only did he have to mediate the dispute between the two boys, he had to purchase two new sets of rims! Whenever we quarrel with each other in the body of Christ, it is our heavenly Father we are hurting. If we fail to act in peace with each other, it is a reflection on Him. Perhaps this is why Paul urged believers to "be at peace among yourselves" (1 Thessalonians 5:13).

Conflict was prominent in many of the early churches since both a

Jewish and a Gentile faction existed. For centuries there had been a massive barrier of religious and cultural animosity between God's chosen people, Israel, and those whom they regarded as pagan Gentiles. The hatred and mistrust that grew from this enmity was evident, even in dealings within the church. It was that specific conflict as well as conflict between Christians of different races, different social and cultural backgrounds, different nationalities, and other kinds of division that Paul addressed when he pointed out, "For He Himself is our peace, who has made both one, and has broken down the middle wall of separation" (Ephesians 2:14).

But can this reconciliation have an impact on the church in our twentieth century world of racial animosity, ethnic cleansing, and riot-torn cities? Without question it can! Here are two contemporary illustrations of God's reconciling power at work.

Ed and Lana were part of what might be described as a "lily white" church in a small town in Texas. They had both been raised to distrust people of other races, particularly African-Americans and Hispanics. The community in which they lived, raised their children, and managed a small family business was marked by an uneasy truce between Anglos, Hispanics, and African-Americans—a truce occasionally broken by various hostile incidents.

When Ed's pastor and several other area ministers began planning a county-wide evangelistic outreach at a local stadium, Ed was one of the first to voice his opposition to anyone but whites participating. Many who were part of the crusade planning team agreed, while others felt equally as strong that anyone—regardless of race—should participate. Ed's pastor and others prayed, and God worked in the hearts of all those who became involved. As Ed's pastor would later describe it, "It was one of the high points of my ministry. I was standing outside the stadium that first evening of the crusade while Ed was standing with one of the ushers. I'll never forget the smile on Ed's face. When the first African-American family drove up, he went out to greet the man and his wife, welcomed them warmly, then invited them to come in and sit with him and Lana." God had brought reconciliation.

The second incident occurred during the Promise Keepers gathering in another city in Texas in 1994. Harvey, an African-American from Texas who admitted to his anger toward whites, described to the audience of the *Life Perspectives* radio call-in program how God had changed his heart and the hearts of many others through the challenge of one of the Promise Keepers' speakers to seek racial reconciliation. "He challenged us to get together—whites, blacks, members of other races—in small groups, to talk with each other, and to pray together. I wasn't comfortable with the suggestion. I didn't want to. But I talked with the friend I was with, and we decided to give it a try. I couldn't believe it when we ran into a white brother from our community that I had been upset with. We were part of the small group that prayed together. I can't believe how different that made me feel about him and about white brothers in general. It really helped me understand that God is colorblind. We'll all spend eternity together anyway. So we might as well get together here on earth."

That's the kind of practical, life-changing reconciliation the heavenly Father provided when He sent His Son to be the Savior of the world. And just as the father in the parable of the prodigal served as a catalyst for reconciliation, each of us who has experienced God's gracious forgiveness can be a reconciler of others.

The Right Kind of Father

There is another important lesson we need to draw from the father whose story Jesus told. This first-century father provides a superb role model for twentieth-century fathers.

Unfortunately, even with years of family and parenting books, seminars, and the modern Christian men's movement, many men still struggle with this business of fathering. Both of us have talked with numerous men who are committed Christians, who are hard-working, and who have strong moral convictions but who simply aren't cutting it in their important relationships with their children.

While this book isn't designed to be a manual on fathering, there are some good principles in this parable that can help us be the kind of fathers this Jewish man was to his two sons.

First, it is imperative that we love our children unconditionally. Sadly, this is one of the most difficult areas for us to pull off as fathers. Perhaps that's the reason why Paul specifically warns fathers not to embitter their children so that they become discouraged (Colossians 3:21). The father of the prodigal clearly provided a flesh-and-blood example of how unconditional love reaches out to both rebellious and self-righteous children.

Second, as fathers we have a responsibility to provide two important elements our children need in order to develop mentally, emotionally, and spiritually. One is nurture, the positive instruction based on the Bible that every child needs to grow and mature. The other is admonition—the rebuke, discipline, and the appropriate correction every child has to have in order to cope with the effects of sin. Paul combined these two ingredients in his instruction to parents, specifically to fathers, as he concluded his letter to the church at Ephesus (Ephesians 6:4). As we mentioned before, both of our own fathers took the time to instruct us in biblical truth, and neither was hesitant to exercise appropriate discipline. Both of us heard—and felt—the truth of the proverb that reminds us, "Foolishness is bound up in the heart of a child; the rod of correction will drive it far from him" (Proverbs 22:15).

Third, it is essential for fathers to set the example of spiritual leadership in the home. This includes such givens as making a close relationship with God a vital priority in our own lives, including personal and family devotions and faithfulness to church, demonstrating love, respect, and commitment toward our wives, and maintaining an active, loving interest and involvement in the lives of each of our children.

Fourth, it is crucial that we as dads take time—quality and quantity— with each of our sons and daughters. As has so often been asked, how do we best express love to our children? The best way to spell that love is: *time.*

Some years ago a survey was taken involving a number of middle-class fathers to determine exactly how much time was spent with their children each day. Each man was asked to estimate the amount of time he had spent each day with his young children. The average of these father's estimates ranges from fifteen to twenty minutes.

However, as a part of the survey, microphones had been attached to the shirts of the children to record the actual amount of interaction between father and child. Incredibly, the average dad spent *thirty-seven seconds* with each child, in an average of less than three daily encounters, generally of ten to fifteen seconds at a time.[2]

It is no wonder that, as pop singer Harry Chapin put it in his poignant ballad "Cat's in the Cradle," the father who had no time for the boy who wanted to grow up to be just like him finally lamented near the end of his life, "My boy was just like me." Preoccupied with business and multiple demands, the son in the song simply had no time for his aging father.

Florida businessman and author Patrick Morley made it a habit to ask older men what their life's greatest regrets were. While the wording varied, Morley recalled two that showed up on virtually every man's list. "First, a man would say 'I was so busy taking care of company business that I never put my own financial house in order. . . .'

"Then he would add, 'I was so busy trying to improve my family's standard of living that, before I knew it, my children were grown and gone, and I never got to know them. Now they are too busy for me.' "[3]

We are not told how much time the father in Jesus' story put into his two sons. We do know that in their point of crisis, he had time for each.

Do we fathers have time for our children?

Reconciliation and Relationship

In this chapter we have taken a somewhat different look at the father of the prodigal son. More than just a character in a story, he is also a role model whose actions deserve our admiration and imitation.

His efforts at reconciling both of his sons to himself and then to each other bring the picture of biblical reconciliation into sharp focus. God has reconciled a rebellious humanity to Himself through the Cross of Jesus Christ. Each of us who has experienced that reconciliation through faith in Jesus can be the means of reconciling people to God and to others. In our strife-ridden and dysfunctional world, such a message of grace, forgiveness, and interpersonal peace has incredible impact!

The second important facet of this father's legacy is his role modeling of a mature parental relationship. While we only have the small vignette Jesus painted for His hearers, we can see how this man models for us the unconditional love, the willingness to both nurture and confront, and the investment of time parents need to make today.

Endnotes

1. *The World at Arms* (London: The Reader's Digest Association Limited, 1989), 30–33.

2. James C. Dobson, *Straight Talk to Men and Their Wives* (Waco, TX: Word Books, 1984), 35–36.

3. Patrick Morley, *The Man in the Mirror* (Brentwood, TN: Wolgemuth & Hyatt Publishers, 1989), 85.

CHAPTER EIGHT

The Listeners:
Truth and the Heart

The Hound of Heaven

I fled Him, down the nights and down the days;
I fled Him, down the arches of the years;
I fled Him, down the labyrinthine ways
Of my own mind; and in the midst of tears
I hid from Him, and under running laughter.
Up vistaed hopes I sped;
And shot, precipitated,
Adown Titanic glooms of chasmèd fears,
From those strong Feet that followed, followed after.
But with unhurrying chase,
And unperturbèd pace,
Deliberate speed, majestic instancy,
They beat—and a Voice beat
More instant than the Feet —
"All things betray thee, who betrayest Me."

—from the poem by Francis Thompson

The story of the prodigal son is familiar to many people who have only a passing interest in the Christian faith. Millions of parents whose children have strayed have found encouragement from this parable as they hoped and prayed for their own prodigal to return. Countless others have been moved by the touching conclusion to what could have been a terrible tragedy.

Yet if we could somehow step back in time to that day in ancient Palestine, slip into the crowd and listen to Jesus tell the story, we would come to an important realization. Jesus did not recount these details just for the benefit of those whose children had become prodigals.

As we glance around the audience, we might wonder which of the individuals standing in the crowd most needed to hear this story. Some people might expect that the tax collectors and common sinners who listened to Jesus on a regular basis were the ones who really needed to hear this story. Certainly they could relate to the prodigal path followed by the younger son and his desperate need to return to his loving father. Many of them had done just that. Recognizing the error of their ways, they had turned in faith to the heavenly Father who sent His Son to be the Savior of the world.

Others might suspect that the disciples most needed the message of this parable and its two parallels. After all, Jesus had challenged them to carry His message to the "lost sheep" of the house of Israel. As they responded to the call of Christ in their lives, they had shared a deep sense of joy like that of the woman who had discovered her missing coin. Yet they were not the primary targets of Jesus' parable.

Self-Sufficient Scribes and Pharisees

The people who actually needed to hear what Jesus had to say were the men in the crowd—part of an all-male religious fraternity, so to speak—who considered themselves to be religiously self-sufficient and who sensed no need for what Jesus had to say. Luke mentions them specifically—the Pharisees and the scribes.

The Pharisees viewed themselves as the guardians of the Old Testament law. They constantly objected to Jesus' positive response to those they considered clearly beneath their religious or cultural level. The scribes, most of whom were also Pharisees, were a professional class of Old Testament lawyers and legal teachers. They shared the Pharisee's animosity toward anyone they considered to be "sinners." They were also a prominent part of Jewish religious and social life.

We've already examined the scornful attitude, the arrogance, even the intense anger felt by these individuals due to their perception of Jesus' ministry. Our purpose in this chapter is to step back, to gain an overall perspective, and to see why these religious leaders felt such antagonism toward Jesus' message. Why, like the elder brother, did they refuse to rejoice over the return of prodigals to a loving heavenly Father? Why weren't they glad when common people, who had made no effort to live by the standards of the Mosaic Law, acknowledged the error of their ways and turned toward the Lord? Why were they so incensed when tax collectors like Matthew—Jews who had sold out to a corrupt Roman society in order to make money by collecting taxes for the occupying army—responded to Jesus' love? Why did they feel so intensely that Jesus should send these undesirables away and refuse to have further contact with them?

A Contrast of Compassion

There is an amazing contrast between Jesus' attitude toward "common sinners" and the attitude of these self-important scribes and Pharisees. They avoided common people like the plague, while Jesus went out of His way to come in contact with them. The Bible says that the "common people heard Him gladly," in spite of His message which called for a repentant heart and a changed life. They responded to the authentic love they sensed in both His message and His actions.

Clearly, Jesus loved people with problems—both moral and physical. He wasn't afraid to reach out to a woman possessed by a demon, to a man infected with leprosy, or to a woman guilty of adultery. When others told Him not to waste His time on children, He sternly corrected that attitude and then invested His valuable time in personal contact with each little child. When people who came to hear Him were weak from hunger and ready to faint, He miraculously provided for their physical needs.

While Jesus' ministry was permeated with concern for people, the Pharisees had less compassion for others than the moisture content of the West Texas plains after a summer drought. While the Savior's compassion drew Him to fallen, broken people, the Pharisees' response more closely resembled a person with persistent allergy problems locked in a room filled with fresh flowers.

Two factors can be identified at the core of this incredible contrast: each had a different perception of God and each had a different heart or inner person.

God Concept

It's incredible how our concept of God colors our attitude toward people. Over the years, the Pharisees had developed a perception of God as a harsh, cruel taskmaster who expected a great deal from His followers and who had zero tolerance for errors. The idea of a God who was interested in seeking out lost sinners was totally contrary to everything they thought or stood for. From their perspective, it only made sense for God to obliterate tax collectors and sinners.

Jesus, on the other hand, came "to seek and to save that which was lost" (Luke 19:10). As the Son of God, He perfectly represented His loving, seeking heavenly Father. Over and over He offered the invitation of a God who called sinners to a true knowledge of Himself. Day after day, His life backed up that message—to the degree that His adversaries had absolutely no basis to accuse Jesus of even one incident of moral failure (John 8:46). That in itself must have galled these Pharisees.

On this particular day, they must have felt exasperated as they listened to Jesus' parable of the lost sheep and the lost coin. They clearly understood what He was saying because both these missing items were valuable. No effort was spared to recover them, and when they were located, there was a great sense of joy.

They also couldn't miss the thrust of Jesus' pointed application, "Likewise, I say to you, there is joy in the presence of the angels of God over one sinner who repents" (Luke 15:10). These Pharisees wanted nothing to do with a God who cared for anyone other than people like themselves. They only approved of people who performed up to God's exacting standards—which took a lot of personal denial and twisting of the truth, of course! From their perspective, anything else just wasn't good enough.

Then Jesus told the story of the prodigal son.

As the story unfolded, they probably initially felt pretty good about what they were hearing. They correctly understood the prodigal to represent the common sinners and tax collectors with whom Jesus had been associating. Perhaps they thought to themselves, *Finally He's telling a parable that shows how things really are. After all, here's a father being rejected and spurned by a son who was clearly a sinner.*

Then Jesus threw them a curve. He spent the rest of the story discussing the older brother. This turn in the story hit much too close to home—unmistakably, the older brother represented them.

The Pharisees' True Condition

The Pharisees, like the older brother, viewed themselves as always working in order to please God. They did not perceive their relationship with the heavenly Father as one of love but rather of performance. While Jesus had earlier explained the importance of loving God wholeheartedly and loving people unconditionally (Luke 10:25–28), they held themselves in bondage to God and felt snobbish disdain toward other people.

The best description of the Pharisees' religion occurs in the gospel of Matthew. They had carefully crafted an external religion designed to impress others with the dedication of their lives and the value of the service they rendered to God. Jesus, however, graphically observed that theirs was a life of hypocrisy (Matthew 23:13). They didn't really have the righteousness that would qualify them to go to heaven even though they thought they did. Nor were they interested in others being able to go. They were skilled at voicing impressive prayers on the one hand while on the other foreclosing on needy widows for their own personal gain (v. 14). While they actively sought converts to their way of life, what they taught their converts doomed them to eternal judgment (v. 15). While they professed to be able to guide others, their spiritual blindness made such efforts ludicrous (vv. 16–17). While they maintained a focus on external acts of worship, they missed the point of what was truly holy (vv. 18–22). Masters of the "public relations" approach to giving, they missed the matters which were of a far greater weight in God's eyes: justice, mercy, and faith (v. 23).

So Jesus used four powerful images in an effort to drive home the totally inconsistent nature of the Pharisees' professed religious expertise. First, He called them blind guides—and who would seek to be directed by a blind person? Then, He pointed out the inconsistencies in their approach, labeling them as people who would choke on a gnat but swallow a camel. Next, He pictured them as eating and drinking from utensils that were clean on the outside but unspeakably filthy on the inside. Finally, He portrayed them as painted tombs—outwardly beautiful but filled with decaying bodies (v. 27).

The Heart of the Matter

The scribes and Pharisees not only had a different perception of God than Jesus had, but the essential condition of their hearts was different. When we talk about heart disease or heart problems today, we frequently think of coronary surgery and transplants, angioplasty and multiple bypasses. Certainly great strides have been made in helping individuals with physical heart trouble.

Some years ago, noted heart surgeon Dr. Michael DeBakey was walking down a street in his home town of Lake Charles, Louisiana. He spotted a baby in the arms of its mother. Merrill Prater was born a "blue baby" because of the inability of his heart to pump blood through his body. His chances of growing up to live a normal, active life weren't good.

Getting the parents' phone number, Dr. DeBakey set up a meeting at which he offered to perform open-heart surgery on Merrill. After a long period of consideration and discussion, Merrill's parents took the child to Houston where Dr. DeBakey performed what was then a rare operation. Merrill's little chest was opened, a machine took over pumping blood through his body, and his damaged heart was repaired so it could function correctly. The operation not only saved Merrill's life, but it also gave him the ability to live a normal life.

From a spiritual perspective, that's exactly what the Pharisees and scribes of Jesus' day needed and what all the "elder brothers" of our day need as well. The common denominator in each case is a spiritually weak and morally deceptive heart.

The word *heart*, as generally used in Scripture, does not refer to the four-chambered pump located in the chest cavity. Rather, as can be most clearly seen from its use in the Old Testament book of Proverbs, the heart refers to the focal point of the *inner person*. The term *heart* is found almost one hundred times in the English translations of the book of Proverbs. Four different Hebrew words are used; the most common, *lev*, "includes the motives, feelings, affections, and desires . . . also the will, the aims, the principles, the thoughts, and the intellect of man."[1] That's why the author of Proverbs warned his readers, "Keep your heart with all diligence, for out of it spring the issues of life" (Proverbs 4:23).

Like many professing Christians today, the Pharisees were adept at putting all their efforts into maintaining an outward show of religiosity but without any heart reality. That's why they clashed with the Lord Jesus on so many occasions.

On one such occasion, the Pharisees confronted Jesus with what they considered a major complaint. His disciples had been violating a tradition of the elders by failing to engage in the elaborate ritual of ceremonial handwashing prior to eating. The issue was not personal hygiene at mealtime but one of religious ceremony. Knowing their hearts, Jesus confronted them with the inconsistency and hypocrisy of making an issue over relatively unimportant ceremonial manners while failing to practice honesty and integrity. Then He drew the contrast between external appearances and internal realities which they had failed to grasp—a distinction we all need to understand and apply today.

"Not what goes into the mouth defiles a man; but what comes out of the mouth, this defiles a man. But those things which proceed out of the mouth come from the heart, and they defile a man. For out of the heart proceed evil thoughts, murders, adulteries, fornications, thefts, false witness, blasphemies. These are the things which defile a man, but to eat with unwashed hands does not defile a man." (Matthew 15:11, 18–20)

The heart issue is still of fundamental importance today. God's primary interest is not in the external behavior of those who profess to follow Him but in the internal reality of the heart. He wants us to come to Him in repentant faith like the prodigal to his father. Second, He wants us to genuinely care about other people.

How can we know the condition of our own hearts? Both of us have found significant help in the Old Testament book of Proverbs. Since the heart is mentioned frequently in its thirty-one chapters, this book of the Bible describes both the spiritually healthy and the spiritually unhealthy heart.

The Unhealthy Heart

The first principle we see about the unhealthy heart in Proverbs is that it is turned against the Lord. It refuses to obey Him or trust Him. As Solomon compiled these maxims to give his son a treasury of wisdom or skill in living, he established an important principle at the outset: "The fear of the Lord is the beginning of knowledge" (Proverbs 1:7).

The wise king's appeal to his son was "apply your heart to understanding" (2:2); "But let your heart keep my commandments" (3:1); and "Trust in the Lord with all your heart, and lean not on your own understanding" (3:5). The healthy heart, according to Solomon, is one that trusts in the Lord and gives complete obedience to Him. In short, "The wise in heart will receive [God's] commands" (10:8). Unfortunately, our hearts are too often stubborn and self-willed, arrogantly asserting our own way rather than submitting to His way. Such a heart, rebelling against God's commands rather then submitting to them, is headed for spiritual heart failure.

How do we get that way? How do our hearts begin imagining evil? According to Solomon we deceive ourselves for "deceit is in the heart of those who devise evil" (12:20). It is a subtle infection. Like malignant cells it can creep in undetected, multiply over time, and prompt us at points of decision to choose our own way rather than God's. The more we do this, the more we consequently harden our hearts against God's reproof and set ourselves up for personal disaster. "He who hardens his heart will fall into calamity" (28:14).

King David, Solomon's father, had practiced a heartfelt love and trust toward God from his first days as a shepherd. In his early years of difficulty and political adversity and during the first years of his reign as king over Israel, he faithfully followed God's will. Sadly, after he became king, David allowed his heart to decline. Instead of obeying God's command that kings should not multiply wives or military power, he decided it was better to do things his own way. This gradual hardening of his attitude against God, much like the hardening of concrete, left David susceptible to the temptation to commit adultery with the wife of one of his trusted military officers. Then, he carried out a cover-up that included murder.

Why do people, even those of obvious sensitivity to God, become hard-hearted? As the Bible points out, the underlying trigger is the deceitfulness of sin (Hebrews 3:13). This is why we all need daily spiritual accountability as a vaccine against spiritual hardness.

Sometimes we become angry toward God because of some loss in our lives. Other times we think He has failed to deliver something we feel entitled to (Proverbs 14:6). Such bitterness toward God frequently manifests itself in an unwillingness to submit to His guidelines for living. We develop a rebellious and hostile heart toward God.

Raymond had a beautiful wife, two small children, and an active ministry in a local church that included teaching the Bible. Although everything seemed great on the outside, Raymond's heart wasn't right with the Lord. Over a period of years a lack of accountability, a heart filled with bitterness against the Lord, and a refusal to listen to the counsel of others set him up for a spiritual disaster. When Raymond became involved with another woman, he wound up losing his wife and children and walking away from the ministry God had given him. Today he chooses to have very little contact with his former Christian friends and has no interest in spiritual things.

Another indicator of a sick heart is denial. It is a heart that refuses wisdom and understanding. The author of Proverbs called to the uninformed person to understand wisdom and to have an understanding heart (8:5). Unfortunately, as Proverbs 18:2 points out, "A fool has no delight in understanding, but [only] in expressing his own heart." Such an individual seeks only his or her own desires and opinions, refuses to listen to the counsel of God or of others, and ultimately has no concern for gaining the wisdom that teaches one how to live rightly (17:16).

Diana prayed to receive Christ when she was a first-grader. For years, she told anyone who asked that her goal in life was to become a missionary, to tell people of Jesus and His love. After painful exposure to a number of people who chose to preach one thing and live another, Diana became bitter and cynical. Refusing to face or even acknowledge her hurt and bitterness over what had happened, she poured her energies into scientific and intellectual pursuits and became skilled at her chosen field. She chose to reject God and His loving call on her life and allowed those who had offended her to ultimately rob her of the Lord's wisdom and direction. She was operating at two different levels of denial: on one level, she denied the true source of her pain which came from people rather than from God; on the other she refused to face the call to which she had earlier committed herself.

A third characteristic of an unhealthy heart is that it plans and pursues evil. In Proverbs 6:12–14 Solomon describes the worthless, wicked individual whose heart is perverse and constantly comes up with sinful schemes and creates discord among people. Ultimately this person will reap—in sudden, dramatic fashion—the calamity which he or she has sown (6:15). Such individuals have engaged in self-deception, even as they dream up ways to deceive others (12:20). These proud yet perverse hearts are, to paraphrase a proverb, "a stench in the nostrils of God."

J. P.—as he liked to be called—was an admitted deal-maker. There was nothing he enjoyed more than putting together deals, and in the Texas real estate boom of the early eighties he seemed to be at the right place at the right time.

However, when real estate values began to collapse, many of the individuals who had been involved in the partnerships and other "deals" engineered by J. P. discovered just how self-serving those agreements had been. Many of them fell into bitter disagreements with their erstwhile partners, most experienced great financial difficulty, and some even wound up filing for bankruptcy—all while J. P. quickly moved on to other lucrative pursuits. Eventually, the deceitful deals he had made came home to roost, and he lost fortune, family, and reputation—all in one catastrophic event.

Yet even in his fall from wealth and status, J. P. exhibited the final characteristic of the unhealthy heart—arrogance. Refusing to accept personal responsibility, he blamed others and even God, arrogantly proclaiming he had done nothing wrong even in the face of a number of witnesses. The same term for arrogance is used to identify every individual who is proud in heart (Proverbs 16:5). The arrogant look and the proud, swollen heart are labeled by God as sin (21:4). And of all the things listed in Proverbs that are hated by God, none is greater than the proud look that reflects the arrogant heart (6:16–17). Such a heart leads to the arrogant self-reliance practiced by the Pharisees of Jesus' day, a characteristic labeled by God as perverse (28:26).

These scribes and Pharisees, like the elder brother, must have put up a good front. But doing and saying what appeared to be the right things outwardly didn't make the grade. Their hearts needed changing.

As we examine these hard, persistently arrogant hearts, turned against the Lord and fixed in denial and dreaming up evil, we might be inclined to wonder, can such hearts be changed? The answer we discover later in the New Testament is a resounding Yes! Even a hardened, arrogant, self-reliant Pharisee can be transformed.

A Transformed Pharisee

Such a man appears later in the New Testament with the same profile as the Pharisees who stalked Jesus' trail. This man became intensely angry toward those who professed to follow the Christian way. One New Testament historian described him as "breathing out threats and murder against the disciples of the Lord" (Acts 9:1).

By his own admission, he derived both significance and satisfaction from his religious pedigree and the catalog of his activities. His name was Saul of Tarsus, and he made it clear that he had outperformed all others of the Pharisaic persuasion. One's tribal pedigree was a particular point of Jewish pride. Saul could identify his tribe, the Benjamites, a southern tribe which gave Israel its first king, Saul, for whom he had been named. As a "Hebrew of the Hebrews," he had carefully studied and kept the Law. He considered himself to be blameless in all the ceremonial points of Jewish law and righteousness. In addition, he had a burning zeal which drove him to persecute the enemies of Judaism, especially those who had followed what he considered to be the pernicious way of Jesus (Philippians 3:4–6).

Surely, if anyone could have earned merit before God, it was this young, zealous Pharisee. Yet in his zeal to keep the Mosaic Law and persecute those who taught a different way, he proved to be just like the older brother in the story of the prodigal. His was a performance-based relationship with God which in effect constituted no relationship at all.

Everything changed one incredible day as Saul was rushing from Jerusalem to Damascus to carry out his mission of throwing Christians into jail. Somewhere along that road, in dramatic fashion, he met the resurrected Christ (Acts 9:3–5). In the process, he learned that what he had considered service to God was actually a personal attack on the Savior who loved him and died for him.

His life changed by that conversation with the risen Jesus, the one who formerly persecuted Christians now began preaching Christ's message of love and forgiveness (Acts 9:20). As he would later write to believers, "But what things were gain to me, these I have counted loss for Christ. Yet indeed I also count all things loss for the excellence of the knowledge of Christ Jesus my Lord" (Philippians 3:7–8).

What an amazing transformation in the thinking of this model Pharisee! Before, he had sought to justify himself by performance; now, personally related to Christ, he had a right standing with God which he received through faith in Christ (Philippians 3:9).

As a result, his attitude toward people was transformed from arrogant hatred to unconditional love. As he later wrote to the church in Corinth—ironically the church that seemed to have the least respect for his ministry—"It is the love of Christ that grips or motivates me" (2 Corinthians 5:14, paraphrased). Paul's love for the Lord who had loved him enough to die for him so permeated his life that his attitude toward other people was radically changed (2 Corinthians 5:16). Now he was a representative of Christ, begging people from all walks of life to be reconciled to the God who paid for all their sins (vv. 20–21).

Every Person Valued

How Jesus must have longed for these Pharisees and scribes to understand the incredible love God has for every person.

The message that Christ so fervently sought to communicate to the self-righteousness Pharisees was that every individual matters greatly to God the Father. That love, friend, includes you. Perhaps, like the prodigal, you have lived far below God's standard. Or, like the older brother, you may have sought to live by the external standard of human morality, even though you sense that your best efforts aren't good enough. God's forgiveness and grace are yours for the asking. The ultimate message of the prodigal son is that God gave His Son, Jesus, who died and rose from the dead that every individual might become God's adopted child by faith.

So if you haven't done so, why not make this the time when you express your trust in Him. You may choose words something like this:

"Lord Jesus, thank You for dying in my place on the cross and for rising from the dead. I trust You, God's perfect Son, as my substitute who paid the price for my sins. I am trusting You as my only way to heaven. Thank You for saving me and for giving me the free gift of everlasting life."

Endnotes

1.   Robert B. Girdlestone, *Synonyms of the Old Testament* (Grand Rapids: William B. Eerdmans, 1897), 65.

PART TWO

Portraits of Prodigals

Now you've met the prodigal, his father, and his older brother. Perhaps you could identify most strongly with the prodigal. Or you may have found you had more in common with the older brother. Or some may have been through the same heartache and restored hope that the prodigal's father experienced.

There are other prodigals in Scripture we'd also like you to meet. These men and women will help you understand that we all are prodigals in one way or another because of the impact of sin. As Solomon once said, "There is not a just man on earth who does good and does not sin" (Ecclesiastes 7:20).

If Jesus were speaking, He might introduce our first portrait of a biblical prodigal by saying, "I'd like to introduce you to Peter. I'll tell you about his great temptation and his tragic fall. It's a sad story—you might even be tempted to cry.

"But there's a lesson in Peter's story I want you to learn. You too may fall at some point. In fact, there's a good chance that in some way you will.

"But I have a remedy for such falls. You can always turn to Me in repentance and in confession. If you do, I will forgive you and welcome you back to fellowship with great joy. And if you choose not to, you will suffer the consequences. It will cause Me great grief, of course, because I love you."

And Peter is only the beginning. We have a varied collection of biblical characters for you to meet. You'll see the numerous ways they contrived to turn away from the Lord, and you'll be amazed at the marvelous ways God dealt with them to draw them back to Himself.

Perhaps you're wondering at this point *just what is a biblical prodigal? How can you tell prodigal behavior from just plain "garden variety" sinful behavior?* Perhaps the distinction is a subtle one, but it seems to us there are four distinguishing marks of what we call prodigal behavior.

First, a biblical prodigal is one who has experienced some measure of fellowship with God. Just as the prodigal son at one time lived at home in apparent fellowship with his father, so other prodigals have maintained some kind of connection with the Lord.

Second, a biblical prodigal is one who has abandoned that level of fellowship with God. The departure may have been sudden, or it may have culminated a gradual decline in the relationship. But there has been an observable departure similar to what occurred with the wayward son Jesus described.

A third characteristic is that the biblical prodigal experiences either wasteful or harmful consequences. David, for example, experienced personal pain and conflict, brought harm to his family, and disgraced the name of the Lord (2 Samuel 12:10–14).

The fourth trait of a biblical prodigal we have observed is that he or she ultimately returns to fellowship with the Father. Peter's repentance, for example, was evidenced by extreme sorrow. David recorded his own confession in what we now know as Psalm 51.

In summary, biblical prodigals are people who have walked in fellowship with the Lord to some degree, departed from fellowship into wasteful or harmful behavior, and then returned.

Our challenge is to make sure we do not follow their prodigal paths. If we apply the lessons they learned—mostly the hard way—we can draw encouragement from their stories. That's the goal both for those who are prodigals and for those who love them.

CHAPTER NINE

Peter: Fear Leads to Failure

Here lies one who feared God so much that he never feared the face of any man.

—said of John Knox, leader
of the Scottish Reformation

He was one of the most colorful New Testament characters ever to slip on a sandal. He is the only one who ever asked Jesus to let him walk on water. He alone dared to speak up with a suggestion on the frightening Mount of Transfiguration. He was the only disciple so uninhibited as to jump into the cool waters of the Sea of Galilee and swim to shore to meet Jesus. Peter is always listed first among the disciples, and he was usually in the forefront of every activity.

He was frequently outspoken; sometimes he could speak for two divergent viewpoints in almost the same voice. For example, his confession, "You are the Christ, the living God" was almost immediately followed by his insistent rebuke of the Lord for suggesting He would go to Jerusalem and be killed by the chief priests and scribes (Matthew 16:16, 21–22). In response to his impulsive confession, Jesus commended him, "Blessed are you, Simon, son of Jonah. You didn't receive this from flesh and blood, but by revelation from My heavenly Father." Later, Jesus lovingly but firmly confronted Peter's ill-conceived rebuke with a stern retort, "Get behind me, Satan, you are offending Me. You do not consider the things that are of God." Certainly Peter had his ups and downs, and both were frequently occasioned by his willingness to shoot from the lip.

Some would have called Peter the classic type A personality. He was a hard-driving overachiever, a take-charge kind of guy, the kind of person once described by speaker Florence Littauer as "a fun-loving individual who also liked to be in charge and had the most fun when he was in charge."

But it wasn't his colorful personality that ultimately drove Peter to prodigal behavior. Nor was it his obvious gift for leadership. Instead, his failure happened at a moment of time when his self-proclaimed courage forsook him, and he acted out of fear.

The First Emotion

Of course Peter wasn't the first individual to discover that fear and failure are a common mixture. When we turn back to the earliest pages of human history, we discover the first couple God created, crouching in the bushes of Eden's garden, covered with fig leaves. As we examine the scene, we hear the voice of the Lord God calling to Adam, "Where are you?" (Genesis 3:9).

From his hiding place, we detect Adam's timid reply, "I heard Your voice in the garden, and I was afraid because I was naked; and I hid myself."

Understandably, having chosen to disobey God's one direct

prohibition, Adam immediately found himself driven by fear. His mind told him he was physically naked which prompted the fear. That in turn led to an act of the will—hiding himself.

This same chain of events has been playing itself out in human lives ever since. The choice to sin made by every one of us has left us spiritually and morally bare before God. Our natural emotional response to this condition is fear, which prompts us to engage in all sorts of mental and intellectual efforts to cover up—denial, rationalization, avoidance, even projecting the blame for our failures onto others.

All too many of us find ourselves locked in combat with our emotions, unable to deal with them in a healthy fashion. And fear lies at the heart of many of these struggles.

For example, many of us struggle with anger. We cannot control our tempers. We cannot resolve bitterness. One important insight we frequently overlook is that anger is an emotion that grows out of fear, to a large degree.

An illustration from our office explains what we mean. Both of us have worked late in the historic old building in which Back to the Bible was housed in downtown Lincoln, Nebraska, for more than forty years. It is a four-story structure with a basement and many narrow halls, steep stairs, and twisting passageways.

Imagine for just a moment that you have been touring Back to the Bible's building late one evening during the winter when it grows dark early. Suddenly, you discover that you have been left behind by the group you were with. The main lights have been turned out, and only the emergency lighting is on.

Feeling somewhat anxious and apprehensive, you begin trying to find your way out of the building. Suddenly, as you round a sharp corner, you run headlong into someone who responds with just one word.

"Boo!"

What would your initial emotional reaction be? If you were like most of us, you'd be frightened. You might even admit to being scared half-to-death.

What would be the next emotion to which you almost immediately shifted?

Probably anger.

You'd be likely to say something like, "Why did you go off and leave me? How come you were trying to scare me like that?" You could even feel furious. Perhaps you'd be tempted to grab your friend by the shoulders and give him or her a good shaking! At the very least, you'd probably be inclined to give him or her a piece of your mind you couldn't spare!

That's how fear often operates in our lives. Frequently it invades our consciousness at an unguarded moment, prompting us to act in a way that is not only out of control but may be uncharacteristic of our normal behavior patterns. It can cause us to do things that are harmful to ourselves, to others, and even to the cause of Christ.

In short, it can push us toward prodigalism.

Impending Failure

That's exactly what happened to Peter. He and the other disciples had gathered in the second-story room of a house in Jerusalem, eating the Jewish Passover meal and listening to the Lord's warning about things that were to come. Jesus assured them that He would never leave them nor forsake them.

Peter had also heard a chilling warning: "The hand of My betrayer is with Me on the table." At that point he and the other disciples began asking each other who would do such a thing (Luke 22:21–23).

It's likely that many intense emotions were whirling around in Peter's head after the Passover supper. Perhaps his heart swelled with pride as Jesus said, "And I bestow upon you a kingdom, just as My Father bestowed one upon Me, that you may eat and drink at My table in My kingdom and sit on thrones judging the twelve tribes of Israel." Then, as Luke records the conversation, the Lord addressed Peter specifically, calling his name twice to be sure He had his attention. He said, "Indeed, Satan has asked for you, that he may sift you as wheat" (vv. 29–31).

What a comforting and then disconcerting thing to be told! How embarrassing for one who was perceived both by himself and others as the leader of Jesus' trusted band of disciples.

Yet Jesus made it clear to His followers that this wasn't just a warning for Peter. "All of you will be made to stumble because of Me this night," the Savior warned them (Matthew 26:31). In short, He was saying, "All of you will run in fear of your lives and scatter like scared sheep."

Immediately Peter spoke up, "Even if all are made to stumble because of You, I will never be made to stumble" (v. 33). To Peter, such a failure on his part was inconceivable. He just couldn't accept even a hint that he might fall. He paid no attention to Jesus' warning. Without hesitation, he contradicted the Savior. When the going got tough, the other disciples might turn tail and run. That wouldn't surprise him, but not the big fisherman, not Simon Peter—to run from trouble just wasn't his style.

Furthermore, Peter loved Jesus. He cared about Him deeply. He was convinced Jesus was the Messiah. Surely his feelings of love and loyalty toward Jesus could carry him through any kind of temptation.

The Overconfidence Trap

Have you ever been there? Have you ever found yourself tempted to think there was no temptation that could trap you, that you would never violate your moral principles? As a Christian, have you felt that no competing passion could draw you away from loyalty to Jesus, no feelings could overshadow your love for Him? That's the kind of attitude the Bible warns us against when it says, "Let him who thinks that he stands take heed lest he fall" (1 Corinthians 10:12).

When the Dallas Cowboys earned their first Super Bowl victory of the 1990s, the game turned into a rout in the second half. One of the Cowboys' up-and-coming defensive stars was a behemoth of a tackle named Leon Lett. Commended by his coach for both his quickness and his fierce tackling style, Lett found himself in the enviable position of scooping up a fumble and running unimpeded toward the goal line with not a blue Buffalo jersey in sight. As he crossed the 10-yard line, en route to his supreme moment of triumph before tens of thousands of screaming fans in the stadium and tens of millions more on worldwide television, Leon held the ball aloft in celebration as he prepared to cross that final stripe. Then, just as he reached the one-yard line, wide receiver Herman Beebe—perhaps the fleetest member of the Buffalo offensive team—rushed up from behind and swatted the ball away. Instead of a Leon Lett touchdown, there was a touchback, and Buffalo regained possession of the ball.

It was a defining moment of supreme humiliation snatched from the jaws of impending triumph. It vividly illustrates the principle that Peter failed to heed: the moment we least expect it, we are the most vulnerable to temptation.

Quite often, that temptation will be prompted by fear.

Spiritual Watergate

Both of us have flown into Washington, D.C., on many occasions. Usually we land at National Airport, which is the closest to downtown. Located on the banks of the Potomac River, easily visible from an aircraft landing or taking off to the northwest, is an impressive semicircular structure adjacent to the distinctive Kennedy Center for the Performing Arts. It is the Watergate Apartment Complex, and its name has become synonymous with shame, disgrace, and failure of the highest magnitude. It was through a seemingly inconsequential burglary that occurred in the Watergate complex that a president of the United States was forced to do what none of his predecessors had ever done: resign from office in humiliation rather than face impeachment.

There's a sense in which Peter experienced a spiritual Watergate. Judas had already succumbed to Satan's deceptive power, and now Jesus pointed out to Peter, "Satan has asked for you that he may sift you like wheat." Satan had sought to bring this leader of the disciples through an intense trial. Within the gracious sovereignty of God, permission had been granted. Just as wheat in Peter's day might be winnowed by being tossed in the air from a circular, woven sifter, so Peter would be put through an intense test in the impending winds of adversity (Luke 22:31).

Even though Satan would put great pressure on Peter, the provision of Christ would be greater. Jesus emphasized, "But I have prayed for you, that your faith fail not."

Christ's Intercession

Several important observations surface from Christ's intercessory ministry on behalf of Peter and the other disciples. The first of these can be seen from the word Jesus used. He did not employ the most common word for prayer which simply meant to ask or inquire (Luke 5:13; 14:18–19; 16:27). Nor did He use another common word for prayer used seven times in Luke to describe the prayer life of Christ, a word which denotes prayer in the context of an active relationship.

Instead, the term Jesus employed was the word frequently translated "beseech." Its root meaning focuses on a lack or need, and it looks at the object for which the prayer is offered. In Peter's case, the reason for using this particular word is evident. He had a need, a weakness of which Jesus was clearly aware, even though Peter was still caught up in denial.

It's encouraging to know that Jesus is fully aware of all our needs and our weaknesses. As the author of Hebrews promised, He continues to make intercession before God on our behalf. His presence at the Father's throne is clearly for our benefit. His ministry of prayer and His accessibility to us when we pray provide an incredible motivation for us to hold fast rather than waver as Peter did (Hebrews 7:25, 9:24, 4:14–16).

The perfect tense of the verb Jesus used to describe His intercessory prayer for Peter demonstrated that this was not a "one-shot" prayer voiced on behalf of His self-confident follower. The point of the prayer is clear as well. Jesus didn't pray that Peter would not be sifted or shaken. He would experience turbulent times. But the Lord's primary goal was that Peter's faith not be eclipsed. Ultimately, Jesus' prayer was answered, even though Peter failed to avail himself of the courage and strength the Lord made available to keep his faith from being overshadowed.

An eclipse is an amazing event. Some time ago, we were standing in the office of a colleague shortly before noon. In the middle of a discussion, someone noted, "Why is it getting so dark?" Then we all remembered that this was the day a solar eclipse was to occur. The moon would pass between the sun and the earth, creating an eerie twilight in what was normally the brightest time of the day. The eclipse lasted for several minutes; then eventually the moon moved on, and the sun's rays once again shown on the city of Lincoln in full force.

Even though the spiritual eclipse brought a time of darkness to Peter's life—a period of prodigal failure—ultimately God's purpose was fulfilled in Peter's life. Not only did he turn back to the Lord himself, but also he fulfilled Jesus' request: "When you have returned to Me, strengthen your brethren" (Luke 22:32).

An Anatomy of Failure

What precipitated the failure on Peter's part? How did it happen that this faithful follower committed the ultimate act of disloyalty—denying even knowing Jesus? We are convinced that tracing the steps to Peter's shocking denial of Jesus can help us avoid succumbing to the same kind of temptation.

The first step in Peter's failure is that he spoke and acted hastily, showing a reckless self-confidence. He refused to listen to the Lord's warning. He didn't ask what it meant or say, "How can I avoid failing?" Instead, with his customary bravado he asserted, "Lord, I am ready to go with you both to prison and to death" (Luke 22:33).

Before we rush to condemn Peter, we need to remember that Mark records that all the disciples spoke in the same way (Mark 14:31). Another detail provided by Mark (and perhaps supplied by Peter) is that Peter emphatically asserted, "Though others will be offended, I will not." Even after Jesus warned Peter that he would deny Him three times before the crowing of the rooster (Luke 22:34), Peter continued to vehemently deny that he would in any way disown the Lord, even to the point of death (Mark 14:31).

Although self-confidence can be helpful in some situations, in others it can be disastrous. Peter's hasty boast of his own commitment did him no favors. Instead, it set him up for a catastrophic failure.

One of the most important lessons we can learn from this prodigal episode in Peter's life is the folly of asserting that it won't happen to me. When we think we are standing the firmest is when we need to pay close attention in order to avoid falling to temptation.

Several years ago, I (Don) was speaking at a Bible conference in Colorado. One of the men attending the conference owned a small, single engine plane. He and his family had flown to the conference from Texas in the plane, and he offered an aerial tour of the beautiful mountains in and around Crested Butte. After climbing to an altitude of approximately five thousand feet, the pilot set out on a course between two mountains. Then he asked, "Have you ever had your hand on the controls of a plane while it was flying?" My affirmative reply was an honest one, but the pilot didn't give me an opportunity to explain just how limited that experience was. He quickly continued, "Here. Hold the controls while I find this chart on the back seat."

Now when someone hands you the controls of a Cessna 180 and you're moving between two mountain peaks, both of which are taller than your current altitude, self-confidence alone doesn't cut it. Only experience and skill in flying counts. It would have been foolish to say, "Sure, I can handle the plane. I'll even land it." Such an assertion would have been fatal. So I wisely offered to look for the chart, instead!

How easy it is for us to rely on a shallow self-confidence to forget how inadequate we really are. How tragic the consequences of such forgetfulness!

Al was a successful businessman and active in his church. He had a vivacious wife and three beautiful children. He and his wife, Rhonda, had a close relationship. They even prayed together on a regular basis.

Al's friend Charlie frequently asked, "How does being on the road affect your spiritual life?"

Al always replied, "No problem. I can handle any temptation that comes my way."

Then one day it happened. Al was away on an extended trip. Days of protracted meetings and hours in a lonely hotel room took their toll, leaving him weak and vulnerable. As he later admitted in shame to his friend, "It was just a one-night stand." He didn't think anybody would ever know, but he wound up catching a sexually transmitted disease which he passed on to his wife. He had been sure he would never fail, but his marriage and his faith were severely tested because he had underestimated the power of temptation and overestimated his ability to cope.

Sleeping at Prayer

That's exactly the kind of bravado Peter expressed. Afterwards he demonstrated just how weak he really was. He and his two associates, James and John, were asked to watch and pray with Jesus. Mark records how Jesus, after agonizing in prayer with His Father, returned and found them sleeping. He sorrowfully asked Peter, "Simon, are you sleeping? Could you not watch one hour?" Then He warned them all, "Watch and pray lest you enter into temptation. The spirit indeed is willing, but the flesh is weak" (Mark 14:37–38).

Some time ago, two friends of ours were driving from one speaking engagement to another. Both were tired because of their busy schedule, and for just a moment, the driver dozed off. In just that short space of time, the car ran off onto the median. When the driver awakened and tried to return to the roadway, the car overturned. The driver suffered serious injuries; the passenger was not quite as seriously hurt. Yet both experienced pain for quite some time afterward. This mishap served as a vivid reminder of just how serious the consequences of falling asleep can be.

That accident illustrates another of Peter's steps toward prodigal behavior. It was natural, when the driver awakened, to pull impulsively at the wheel and jerk the car quickly back on course. For Peter, suddenly awakened from slumber, his first reaction was to draw a sword and, before anyone could respond, cut off the right ear of the high priest's servant (Luke 22:50).

Before you express amazement at Peter's poor skill with a sword, just remember he was a fisherman not a soldier. It is probable that Peter—still lethargic from his sleep, stunned by the multitude, and hearing the question from his fellow disciples, "Lord, shall we smite with the sword"—responded instinctively and tried to split the head of the man nearest him. The fact that he missed at just the right distance to cut off the man's ear was an evidence of the sovereign grace of God. This was further reinforced by the Lord's gracious action in healing the injured man's ear (Luke 22:51).

If you've ever done anything rash or impulsive that you later regretted, you can't help but identify with this third step toward prodigalism. Of course, if you've ever sensed the Lord's forgiveness and grace in dealing with your impulsive failures, you can relate even more with Peter's experience.

We must strenuously avoid becoming complacent and unaware of the danger of prodigal behavior. We may not physically fall asleep as Peter did, yet many people have become indifferent toward the possibility of falling into sin. We must also recognize that an impulsive knee-jerk reaction to circumstances may put us at greater risk of spiritual failure.

Jesus' compassionate miracle of restoring the ear of the man Peter wounded should have been the signal the apostle needed to get his attention. But instead of fulfilling the kind of bold commitment he had voiced earlier, Peter took the fourth of his prodigal steps—he played it safe and followed "at a distance" (Luke 22:54).

Admittedly, it's hard to build an extensive case for spiritual failure on one phrase. After all, the other disciples except for John had forsaken the Lord and fled. They were nowhere to be found. At least when Jesus was taken to the high priest's home in the middle of the night, Peter did follow. We should give him credit for that.

However, there's a principle that anyone who has ever competed in organized sports has heard over and over again. When you are involved in competition, the safest thing to do is to give 100 percent. The competitors who are most likely to be injured are those who, either because of exhaustion, fear, or caution, slack off and try to protect themselves. Athletic experts agree: the individual going less than full speed, showing less than an all-out commitment, is the most likely to suffer an injury.

That seems to be what happened with Peter. He seemed to have taken the safe way, which led to the fifth step down the prodigal path. He sat down with the wrong crowd.

Picture the scene. It's early spring, the middle of the night, undoubtedly chilly as evenings generally are in Palestine at that time of the year. A fire had been kindled in the courtyard of the high priest's residence. Many people were seated there, and Peter sat down among them. These people were not followers of Jesus. They were part of the group that had arrested Him. And out of comfort or expediency, Peter decided this was the place to sit down, rest for a time, and wait to see what happened.

As we should all know, there's danger in hanging out with the wrong crowd. As Solomon warned, "He who walks with wise men will be wise, but the companion of fools will be destroyed" (Proverbs 13:20).

An old proverb says that a man is known by the company he keeps. Or, in this case, Peter was known in contrast to the company he kept. One of the young girls spotted him, looked at him carefully, and said, "He was with Him" (v. 56). Everyone present understood what this girl was saying. Peter was being identified as one who had been with Jesus.

So here was Peter—who had self-confidently boasted, "I'll never desert You, Lord," who fell sleep when he should have stayed alert and prayed, who impulsively pulled his sword and sought to attack when he should have waited for direction from his Lord, who carefully followed at a distance after Jesus was arrested, and who had seated himself with the opposing crowd for the sake of warmth and comfort—now allowing his prodigal direction to take full bloom. As Luke put it, "But he denied Him saying, 'Woman, I do not know Him'" (v. 57).

Striking, isn't it? The same mouth that framed the words "I will never deny you, Lord, I am ready to go with you to prison and to death" is now in effect saying, "Jesus who?"

Moments later, another bystander—this time a man—identifies him as a follower of Jesus. Peter's response is an instant replay of his initial reaction, "Man, I am not!" (v. 58).

An hour passes, nothing happens. Perhaps Peter grew sleepy again. Then suddenly, another of those standing nearby says, "I know it for sure. This individual was with Him. He's a Galilean."

Firmly, and with an oath, Peter responds, "Man, I don't what you're talking about."

When we read this, we react almost in shocked amazement. Why, this is the individual who brashly guaranteed spiritual victory like a cocky NFL quarterback. Then, without warning, a rooster crowed, and the Lord turned and gazed at Peter. Suddenly Peter remembered. He realized the magnitude of his failure, and his bravado dissolved into bitter tears as he fled the crowd.

Not the End

Perhaps it was that look from Jesus, that look of sorrow, that gaze that said, "I haven't forgotten you even though you denied Me in My time of torture and disgrace." It must have been burned into Peter's memory for the rest of his life.

Yes, Peter was sifted like wheat in a sieve. Satan had sought to totally devastate this bold disciple. Yet Jesus used this experience to strengthen Peter and purify him from the combination of arrogant, brash pride and underlying fear that left him susceptible to spiritual disaster.

Jesus still wasn't through with Peter. He had a purpose in mind, a service for Peter to fulfill. "When you have returned to Me, strengthen your brothers." What a refreshing thing to learn as we review these events—Peter's prodigal behavior was not irreversible. He would come back.

Peter could have allowed the rest of his life to be overwhelmed with shame, devastated with the knowledge of his failure and the awareness that others knew the degree to which he had failed. Yet instead of wallowing in self-pity or remaining paralyzed by shame and grief over his failure, Peter allowed his sorrow to become the godly kind—the kind that produces repentance.

And this big, bold individual wasn't afraid to shed tears.

Somehow in our society we have made it unmanly to cry. We give lip service to the fact that Jesus wept. We smile and nod about it. But for many men there is a refusal to admit the value of tears. After all, our popular culture has told us that big boys don't cry. So instead of basing our view of tears on biblical reality, we've turned instead to the modern macho view that masculine tears are always a sign of weakness.

Nothing could be farther from the truth.

It seems that Peter's bitter tears became both the source and the evidence of the cleansing the Lord gave his heart—a cleansing he desperately needed. We are convinced they played a key role in his preparation for future service. They evidenced the authenticity of the turn he made from his prodigal path to future service with God.

Everyone who knew Wayne felt he had his life together. He had an outstanding family, a successful ministry, and he was well liked.

But Wayne had allowed an area of weakness to develop in his life, one that deeply hurt several of his colleagues, placed his family in jeopardy, confronted him with his own mortality, and on several occasions almost—but not quite—brought him to the brink of tears.

As he grappled with his own failure and God's forgiveness, Wayne and his wife, Mindy, flew to New York City for a weekend getaway. Through the efforts of a friend, they were able to secure tickets to the Broadway production of *Les Misérables*, the adaptation of Victor Hugo's classic novel. For three hours, Wayne watched the drama unfold. Jean val Jean, the hero, suffers terrible circumstances and personal failure but refuses to become embittered. Wayne watched the hero's growing faith which came to a climax in a deathbed prayer of confession, acknowledgment, forgiveness, and anticipation of heaven. The emotional dam in Wayne's heart finally burst. As he sat in the balcony of that Broadway theater, his eyes flooded with tears. For the first time since he was a child, Wayne wept until he could weep no more.

Just like Peter, his forgiveness and his cleansing were emotionally reinforced by the release of tears.

Spiritual Landmarks

Those tears became a significant spiritual landmark in Peter's life, but not the only one. Another would occur just after the Resurrection when he would rush to Jesus' grave, go into the tomb, find it empty, and realize how his faith had been confirmed. Still another turning point must have taken place when Jesus actually appeared to Peter individually (1 Corinthians 15:5).

One of Peter's most important landmarks, however, occurred in the final chapter of John's gospel. Peter was tempted to return to his fishing career on the lake of Galilee. Thomas, Nathaniel, James, John, and two of the other disciples went with Peter, and that night they caught absolutely nothing—an incredibly poor performance for such a group of professionals. The next morning, as the mists of dawn cleared, they spotted Jesus standing on the shore although they didn't recognize Him. "Have you caught any fish?" He asked.

"No."

"Why don't you try on the right side of the boat? You'll find fish there." Incredibly, they caught a net full of fish—a net so heavy they couldn't drag their catch into the boat. John turned to Peter and said, "It's the Lord."

Hearing this, Peter wrapped his robe around himself, jumped into the sea, and swam to shore. When the boats reached shore, Peter dragged in the net, filled with one hundred and fifty-three large fish, yet miraculously the net was unbroken. Then, after they had eaten breakfast together, Jesus challenged Peter to feed and shepherd His sheep. He repeated the challenge twice more.

Three times Peter had denied that he knew the Lord. Now three times the Lord asked, "Do you love Me?" Three times He called on Peter to fulfill the shepherd's role.

Despite all he had been through, Peter still struggled with the process. He was grieved because the Lord felt it necessary to repeatedly challenge him about his commitment and love. Yet it took him until the third challenge to express the unselfish commitment of love the Lord was looking for.

Finally, Peter's life and ministry began taking on a new and exciting stability. Bolstered by his personal interaction with the risen Savior, Peter marched across the early pages of the book of Acts, boldly proclaiming Christ to multitudes and individuals alike.

Even though at times he lapsed into failure—the apostle Paul found it necessary to confront him over inconsistency (Galatians 2)—Peter nonetheless became known for the boldness to stand for Christ. In Acts 4:13, the Spirit-inspired courage he and John demonstrated caused those who observed them to note that "they had been with Jesus."

Peter had failed, but Jesus never gave up on this prodigal. Ultimately, Peter began to develop the character Christ had wanted to see in his life when He said of him, "You are Peter [a little rock] and on this rock [of growing and confident faith] I will build My church" (Matthew 16:18).

Significantly, the final words from the pen of this often-impulsive disciple constituted a call to stability. He wrote to those who became his "sheep" to spiritually feed, "But grow in the grace and knowledge of our Lord and Savior Jesus Christ" (2 Peter 3:18). Peter's faith was restored, and he fulfilled the will of Christ for his life as he strengthened his Christian brothers and sisters.

Perhaps the most important lesson we can learn from Peter is that God's grace can restore us even when we have blatantly and thoroughly failed. His strength can enable us to return to fellowship and spiritual growth.

CHAPTER TEN

David: Entitlement Leads to Entanglement

Truth will come to light; murder cannot be hid long.

—Shakespeare, *The Merchant of Venice*

Early May, 1994, marked the death of the man many described as the strongest, most visible U.S. president of the twentieth century. Richard Nixon left his mark on the lives of Americans in numerous ways. Described by friend and foe alike as perhaps the most able president of the modern era in foreign policy, he initiated the Geneva Peace Accords to conclude the war in Vietnam and forged new agreements with the former Soviet Union. Then, through his personal initiative, long-term barriers with China were broken down.

These and other political achievements were mentioned by American political noteworthies ranging from President Bill Clinton to Senator Robert Dole at Mr. Nixon's funeral service, which was held before a watching nation in front of the modest house where Richard Nixon was born. Dr. Billy Graham used the occasion to present a simple message of hope through personal faith in Jesus Christ.

Yet throughout the time between Richard Nixon's death and his funeral—and even during the interim activities themselves—several television commentators simply couldn't resist calling attention to the one word most commonly used to describe Richard Nixon's greatest failure, the word that was associated with his shameful resignation from office.

Watergate.

In the previous chapter, we witnessed the prodigal behavior of one of the most passionate New Testament characters, Simon Peter. David, king of Israel, could certainly be considered his Old Testament counterpart: a man loved and identified with by many, gifted and respected for multiple talents, a brave leader in battle, a sweet singer of hymns of praise, and a man who rose from obscurity to become the greatest ruler in all Israel's history. Most importantly, the Bible characterizes David as "a man after His own heart" (1 Samuel 13:14).

Just as modern historians have acknowledged Richard Nixon's foreign policy triumphs, biblical historians have long recognized David's incredible national leadership and foreign policy skills.

These can perhaps best be summarized in the singular triumph that crowned the early stages of David's life. It's an event easily recalled by referring to the name of the man sometimes called "the most well-known pagan in Scripture."

Goliath.

It must have been an incredible scene—young David striding purposefully down the Valley of Elah toward the mammoth, armor-clad Philistine. David was armed with only a sling and five smooth stones gathered from a nearby brook. The picture has been etched in the minds of just about every boy and girl who ever attended a Sunday school class.

David's amazing victory over Goliath made him an overnight hero in the nation. Almost single-handedly, David had obliterated a decade-long threat to Israel's national security. As a result, the humble shepherd boy was given a position of authority over Israel's men of war and access to the king himself. In addition, he became a close friend with the crown prince, Jonathan, one of the most-respected people in the nation.

Like Richard Nixon, David was a man of many strengths.

There was another way David resembled America's thirty-seventh president. He struggled with a major character flaw, a personal weakness which contributed greatly to his decline in later years. David's weakness involved a deadly combination: a lack of personal accountability, an intense passion, a lack of discipline, and a sense of entitlement. Like a combination of gasoline, gunpowder, and a lighted match, this mix of weaknesses proved volatile, leading to a major personal disaster at a time when David should have been at the zenith of life, spiritually and in every other way.

Just as we summarized David's early triumph with the word *Goliath*, so also a single word can be used to summarize his most colossal failure. It's the word you would expect Hollywood to associate most commonly with David.

Bathsheba.

Just as Watergate came to stand for the decline and fall of Richard Nixon, dogging him until his dying day, so David's moral failure with the wife of one of his military officers, Uriah, has left its stain on the incredible record of the "man after God's own heart."

Chosen and Faithful

Several factors in David's early success are evident from his life, not the least of which was his faithfulness in seemingly small things. Success with little things started with faithfulness in keeping the sheep entrusted to him by his father. His success in facing the challenge of Goliath was followed by success in handling the long-term challenge posed by the paranoid, hostile King Saul. Humanly speaking, these all helped to prepare David for his ultimate role as king of Israel.

However, as Psalm 78 summarized it clearly, it was God who took David from the sheepfolds and who brought him "to shepherd His people Israel." His faithfulness, humanly speaking, followed God's choice. For seven years David ruled in Hebron over the southern tribes of Judah; then he moved his throne to the geographic center and high point of the land, Jerusalem—a site which became known as the City of

David (2 Samuel 5:9). For thirty-three years he reigned there in great power and splendor, enjoying the blessing of the Lord God.

During this time, David's accomplishments were unique and noteworthy. He unified the nation, drawing together the diverse interests of the southern and northern tribes. During the early years of his kingdom, he was a fighting king, a man of war. He and his elite troops subdued the nation's enemies and expanded national boundaries to their greatest extent ever, an area encompassing some sixty-thousand square miles. The psalms he wrote provided significant spiritual impact, drawing the nation toward God.

From a divine perspective, David had been chosen. Humanly speaking, his faithfulness evidenced the unquestioned wisdom of God's choice of this man to lead the people of the Lord. Thus David's success grew out of God's choosing him to lead and his faithful response even in little things.

Humble and Authentic

Another facet of David's spiritual success was his humility. Psalm 78:70 describes David as "His servant." Throughout his life, David willingly and faithfully served his Lord. He always recognized that God was ultimately in charge, just as near the end of his own life he reminded his son Solomon (1 Chronicles 28:9).

Third, David was a man of personal integrity. Psalm 78:72 explained how he shepherded Israel "according to the integrity of his heart." In a world sadly lacking in spiritual focus, personal humility, and authentic integrity, David continues to stand as a shining role model for men and women, even at the end of the twentieth century.

Despite all this, King David still wound up as a middle-aged prodigal.

Time after time, political commentators, newspaper columnists, and people from all walks of life asked, "How could Richard Nixon, the president of the United States, cover up a cheap burglary? How could the Watergate break-in and subsequent cover-up have happened?" Despite the long and intense protestations that he knew nothing about it, an almost universal belief to the contrary ultimately forced him from office.

And how could David, who had a heart for God, holding the awesome position as the king of Israel, with a palace full of beautiful wives, wind up lusting after Bathsheba? Perhaps the only thing we can say is, "No one is immune from spiritual failure or from becoming a prodigal." Since David was king of Israel, it seems appropriate for us to say he blew it royally.

Chuck Colson, former power broker in the inner circle of the Nixon White House and today a leader in the evangelical Christian community, often quotes Lord Acton's dictum: power tends to corrupt, and absolute power corrupts absolutely. One reason for this is that those who hold such power are seldom held accountable for their actions. Certainly from a human perspective, David held absolute power in Israel. He was accountable to no one. Who would challenge him?

Certainly his friend Joab didn't. Joab had been one of David's closest and longest associates after the death of David's best friend, Jonathan. He should have called David's hand and held him accountable. He should have confronted him when he found out what David had done and how he was attempting to cover it up. Joab not only failed to encourage David to do what was right, he actually made it possible for him to continue to do wrong.

Students of human behavior today would probably describe this as *enabling codependency*. They might call it a codependent conspiracy of evil, a compounding of sinful behavior. Just as the Nixon inner circle conspired to allow the cover-up of a variety of wrongdoings at the highest levels of the Nixon presidency, so Joab deceived and manipulated circumstances with callous disregard for the life of one of his own close colleagues, Uriah the Hittite. The results were tragic. Joab failed his king and friend at a critical point. Such failures can be disastrous in our day as well.

For more than a year, Bob and Dick had been part of a small group of men who met together regularly for Bible study and personal accountability. Bob began to notice how often Dick found excuses not to attend. Soon other telltale signs began to appear. One day Bob ran into Dick at a coffee shop in a nearby hotel, seated with a strikingly attractive brunette. Although his friend was married to a blonde, he didn't even ask what was going on. When the two men were out for lunch together, he began noticing Dick would order a cocktail, then two or sometimes three. Before long, Dick's marriage failed and he lost his job. "I just don't understand what happened to him," Bob said, oblivious to the fact that he never passed along any warning or concern.

It's important to remember that David's failure didn't occur as an isolated incident. Its seeds were sown much earlier in his life and grew to bear fruit in an atmosphere of little or no accountability.

From Obscurity to Entitlement

King David began his career in extreme obscurity as a shepherd, the youngest son who didn't seem to matter to his father. He gained respect and notoriety because of his heralded victory over the giant Goliath of Gath. The entire nation recognized his heroism, yet he wound up spending years fleeing from the paranoid wrath of King Saul, hunted down like a common criminal, day after day. Then, almost overnight, David became king.

In Psalm 78 the Bible says that God took David from shepherding sheep to become the shepherd of the nation Israel. With integrity of heart and skillfulness of hand, David led Israel from age thirty through the next forty years of his life.

David had become a man after God's own heart, a man who enjoyed an intimate walk with God and who expressed that fellowship in writing many of the Hebrew songs of praise contained in the book of Psalms.

Yet walking closely with God didn't keep David from feeling entitled to fulfill his own fleshly passions. His first wife, Michal, became a pawn in the conflict between David and her father, King Saul. She was eventually given in marriage by Saul to another man. After his separation from Michal, David married Ahinoam, a resident of Jezreel. Then he took still another wife, Abigail, a woman of personal charm, wisdom, and great physical beauty.

David added wives during his time in the desert and while ruling in Hebron. When he established his kingdom in Jerusalem, he continued to expand his harem, and his lust never seemed to be satisfied. Perhaps David was driven by some personal pain from his childhood or from the time he was pursued by Saul. Perhaps David felt—like so many successful and wealthy individuals in our own day—that God's moral laws didn't apply to him. Yet ultimately it must have been the depravity of his own heart—a depravity just like that found in all our hearts— that caused the king to feel entitled to fulfill his sexual passions.

Earlier in the Old Testament the nation's great leader Moses had warned Israel that a king should never multiply wives, horses, or wealth because they would turn his heart away from the Lord (Deuteronomy 17:16–17). It was a warning David conveniently ignored over a period of slow yet persistent personal decline.

The kingdom of Israel reached its highest point under David and his son Solomon. The kingdom not only included what would become the separate nations of Judah and Israel, but it also included the surrounding kingdoms of Ammon, Moab, Edom, Aram-Damascus, and Aram-Zobah. Israelite governors served in neighboring Damascus and Edom (2 Samuel 8:6, 14). In addition, vassal kings paid allegiance to Israel in Philistia and the Transjordan. The dominion of Solomon was described as including the entire region west of the Euphrates from Tiphsah to Gaza, a huge chunk of the Fertile Crescent (1 Kings 4:24).

War and Failure

During this period, the Ammonites proved to be a continual thorn in the side of the king. Every spring, after the rainy season, it was customary for kings to go into battle (2 Samuel 11:1). The Ammonites, descendants of Lot, lived east of the Jordan River. Their capital, Rabbah, was located approximately thirty miles east of the Jordan River, near the site of modern-day Amman. Their religious rites included the sacrifice of infants to the god Molech. Although it was customary for kings to personally lead their troops into battle, David commissioned Joab to take charge and decided to stay home in Jerusalem.

The biblical text gives no reason for David's decision to stay home. We can only speculate. Perhaps it was what we call a mid-life crisis. Maybe the king simply felt he had served his time at war. Certainly over the course of many years he had fought a considerable number of battles. Perhaps his resolve and commitment to the task of leadership was beginning to wane.

In taking himself out of the front line of battle, he succumbed to a far more insidious and dangerous risk at home. People who play it too safe take the greatest risks. During World War II, psychologist Paul Torrance studied U.S. aces who flew in the Pacific war. He reported that the most obvious characteristic of the ace was his risk-taking ability. They kept testing the limits of their skills. These pilots had fewer accidents and suffered fewer combat casualties than pilots who were inclined to play it safe.

While any or all of those factors could explain the king's behavior, none could excuse what was about to happen. Picture the scene—a warm spring evening. The author of 2 Samuel included more detail than usual, perhaps to show the insidious nature of temptation and the tragic effects of yielding to it. It must have seemed like an insignificant decision when the king arose from his bed in the evening. We might even ask what he was doing in bed at that time. Certainly the king seems to be living proof that an idle mind is the devil's workshop.

From the terraced roof of his luxurious palace, David could enjoy the evening breeze; from its high point in the city, the palace must have commanded a panoramic view of the houses of Jerusalem terraced below him. We are not told what was going through the mind of the king as he enjoyed the view. Perhaps he was bored. Maybe he was thinking about how well things were going for him in the kingdom. Certainly he wasn't prepared for the subtle temptation the Enemy placed in his way, a temptation he failed to resist.

As he looked down, David spotted a woman bathing, probably in a private courtyard near her home. The Bible describes her as stunningly beautiful, and the king immediately wanted her.

How should David have responded to the sudden sight of this woman? Was it a sin even to see her? The answer seems clear from a New Testament writer who described the process of temptation and sin. The sinful action on David's part was not just an accidental glance at a beautiful woman. Every person, the apostle James explains, "is tempted when he is drawn away by his own desires and enticed" (James 1:14). As James notes, there are two ingredients to temptation. There is the "bait," the external enticement, but there is also the internal lust or desire which moves a person to act.

The Process of Lust

Neither of us has a great deal of experience as fishermen, although we have fished with men who are extremely proficient at catching fish. Today's sport fishing is far different from the kind of net fishing practiced by the first-century disciples. For the modern fisherman, the pursuit of bass or trout, bluegill or perch generally involves the use of either live or simulated bait to motivate the fish to strike out of hunger, curiosity, or even anger. Once the fish bites, he discovers to his chagrin the bait is not what it appeared to be at all. Rather than a delightful morsel, its hook proves to be a deadly meal.

This is precisely the kind of process James described when he noted, "Then, when desire has conceived, it gives birth to sin; and sin, when it is full-grown, brings forth death" (James 1:15). His heartfelt warning of verse 16, "Do not be deceived, my beloved brethren," showed his own concern about how this process works and how quickly its fatal consequences can occur.

They certainly happened rapidly for David. Since he was in charge, one of his servants quickly gave him the information he sought: she was married to Uriah the Hittite, one of David's inner circle of trusted soldiers, one of thirty-seven elite members of the king's personal bodyguard. Ironically, Uriah, a convert to Judaism from the Hittites, had been given a Hebrew name meaning "Yahweh Is My Light," a concept about which David himself had written in Psalm 27:1.

None of this mattered to the king or hindered him from sending the messengers to bring her to him. Bathsheba certainly could have resisted the king, although it might have been difficult. The fact is that whatever she did or didn't do, David was the one in a position to say no. Instead, he acted out the desires of his heart, allowing his internal lust to interact with the external attraction, conceiving sin which ultimately led to David's spiritual downfall.

How many times in the lives of God's people has this anatomy of adultery been replayed? Certainly King Solomon's warning, "Keep your heart with all diligence" (Proverbs 4:23), can be viewed as a huge, illuminated sign, flashing out the spiritual warning against the deadly consequences of such behavior. Solomon himself wrote an extended warning against the "immoral woman" (Proverbs 5:3), urging his son to succumb only to the attraction of "the wife of your youth" (Proverbs 5:18). Proverbs 5 warns of the severe consequences—physical, emotional, and spiritual—of immoral behavior.

Certainly in our era, when we hear so much about AIDS and its tragic consequences, such warnings carry an additional ring of authenticity. Yet all too often, in the heat of passion, dire consequences are ignored—with tragic personal and social results.

David certainly knew how to say no to this temptation. He had succeeded in the past, yet his past successes didn't stop him. Even the knowledge that this woman belonged to a man who had camped in the desert with him and had fought by his side didn't hinder him. Of course David knew the commandments of God. He had written songs about God's law. Yet his sense of entitlement and his fierce passion blinded his mind and mastered his body. So he took her, they had relations, and she returned to her home. It was, in modern terminology, a one-night stand.

End of story? Hardly.

Pregnancy and Cover-Up

In a matter of weeks, Bathsheba sent word to David that she was pregnant. This, of course, created a problem for the king since Uriah had been away all this time fighting the Ammonites. David used the brilliant mind with which he had served God to come up with a cover-up plan. Just as in the modern Watergate conspiracy, a foolish act was followed by an attempt to cover the trail. It was prodigal behavior in perhaps its most flagrant form.

David quickly dispatched a messenger to Joab, the commander of his troops, demanding a military briefing from Bathsheba's husband, Uriah. How cool the king must have been as he inquired about his friend and commander, Joab, about the rest of his elite troops, and about the military campaign. How honored Uriah must have felt, how trusting, how unaware of David's tawdry affair with his wife. Then the king dismissed Uriah, suggesting, "Go home. Take a bath. Enjoy the evening." As he left the king's quarters, Uriah even received a gift from David.

All this time, David's mind remained focused on just one thing—getting Uriah back to Bathsheba so they could sleep together. Then when Bathsheba's pregnancy became known, Uriah and others would figure the child was his. Perhaps there would be talk of an early birth, but it would soon go away, and there would be no suspicion of misconduct by the king.

But Uriah, the real hero of this story, was a man of conviction. He wasn't about to go home and enjoy an evening with his wife while the rest of his comrades were sleeping at the battlefront. Instead, he spent the night in the guardroom of the palace with the rest of David's bodyguards. He never went near Bathsheba.

When David found out the next morning, he called Uriah in and with feigned innocence asked why he hadn't gone home. Uriah's reply demonstrated his own integrity, "How could I, in good conscience, sleep in my home, eat and drink my food, and lie with my wife when my captain Joab and my comrades are sleeping in the open field, fighting Israel's enemies and dying?"

Confession or Cover-Up

Even at this point, after attempting to cover his sin, the king could have confessed his wrong and dealt with the consequences of his sin. Instead David moved into stage two of his cover-up. He invited Uriah to spend one more night before returning to the troops, got him drunk, and tried to manipulate him to return to Bathsheba in his drunken condition. Instead, Uriah spent another night with the king's servants. When this desperate plan failed, David sent Uriah back to Joab, carrying his own death notice.

How could the man who wrote so many marvelous songs of praise to God, who had lived a life of such integrity, stoop to carry on like the hero of a modern soap opera or a paperback novel? His prodigal behavior is certainly not unlike others who have been recognized for service to God but who wound up in the web of prodigal behavior. Pastors, Christian workers, and missionaries have all been caught in the same trap of lust and deception with similar tragic consequences.

Al and his wife, Liz, had just built the home of their dreams in the upscale suburban community in which they lived. A successful businessman, Al put a lot of personal time into various stages of construction along with Liz. In the process, they met Phil and Celia, helpful neighbors who volunteered to pitch in during the final phases of construction and clean-up. The two couples began getting together regularly. Soon they even began attending church with Al and Liz, participating in the Bible study class Al taught.

During the finish work on the house, Celia volunteered to help with the painting. During the course of the work, she and Al expressed, then acted on feelings toward each other. Although the two sought to cover-up their relationship and were successful for a time, before long the truth became evident. What began as a dream home ended in a family disaster.

Steps to Failure

How do such moral and spiritual failures develop? In David's case, there were three identifiable steps—all with significant implications for believers today.

First, David's failure began with a lack of personal discipline. At a time when kings were expected to go into battle with their troops, David stayed home. It was unthinkable for the nation's military leader just to stay home and abdicate his responsibility to his people in this way. Imagine a successful football coach like Barry Switzer skipping a Cowboys' play-off game to go fishing. What if Olympic gold medal speed skater Bonnie Blair had decided to go sight-seeing instead of competing in the speed skating finals at Lillehammer in 1994?

David's decision demonstrated a lack of discipline in one area of his life that would have a domino effect in other areas. Having abdicated his military responsibilities, David abdicated his role as the moral leader of the nation as well. Before this, David had obeyed God's commandments with a passionate love. As David's sense of self-discipline relaxed, he was vunerable to a base love of passion itself.

Second, David's feelings were fueled by a sense of entitlement. He looked at this beautiful woman. His gaze became a lingering look, then a fascinated stare, and finally an obsessive lust. She was everything a man could want, and after all, he was entitled to her—he was the king! David's sense of entitlement got him what he thought he deserved, but ultimately cost him more than he could have ever foreseen.

Our own era has been described by many as the "age of entitlement." Over and over the messages of Madison Avenue advertising tell us we're worth it, we deserve it, or "sometimes you have to break the rules." When mixed with temptation, such thinking can be as volatile as gasoline fumes near an open flame.

Third, David's failure was aided by a lack of accountability. Joab should have been the kind of friend who would confront David and ask, "What are you doing sending me orders that will cause one of my trusted men to die? What's going on in your life?" Had he really cared about David, he might have encouraged him to do the right thing and come join the campaign against the Ammonites. But Joab failed to confront the king at this critical point, and neither did anyone else from among David's trusted colleagues.

A True Friend

What David needed at this point was a true friend. Since Joab wasn't a man of moral integrity, God sent along an individual with the courage to face David eye-to-eye.

His name was Nathan, a prophet of God, and he appeared in David's life several months after it must have seemed that the cover-up had been successful. Outwardly, no one could tell what was going on. Yet inwardly, David's feelings were dominated by misery and grief. He couldn't sleep at night. He felt depressed and old beyond his years, even though outwardly he appeared to have a handle on things. The more David struggled to keep his sin hidden, the worse he felt within (David would later describe those intense inner feelings in Psalm 32:3–5).

The adultery was over. Uriah had died, reportedly as a hero in battle. David had said all the right words of encouragement to Joab, voiced the appropriate eulogies for his friend Uriah. Then, when the proper period of mourning had passed, David took Bathsheba as another of his wives, and she gave birth to a son. It seemed things had turned out just as David intended.

But one simple phrase describes how God felt about this sordid incident—"the thing that David had done displeased the Lord" (2 Samuel 11:27).

It was God's love for David and His hatred for His servant's sin that prompted Him to send the prophet Nathan. God had given the king nine months to confess his sin. His heart hardened by his disobedience, David refused to respond to the prompting of his inner misery. Then Nathan arrived, providing a clear example of what true friendship is all about and how loving confrontation can work to restore a prodigal to fellowship with God.

It is significant that Nathan didn't simply launch into a diatribe against David. Instead, he took a powerfully creative and convicting approach. Directed by God, he stirred the king's curiosity with a story about a very wealthy man who had stolen a poor neighbor's pet lamb to provide hospitality for his guests rather than taking an animal from his own extensive flock.

Furious, the king allowed his anger—no doubt a projection of his own guilt—to erupt in a passionate outburst. Going far beyond the Law's demand, David called for the death of whoever had done this thing. Until now, David must have assumed that Nathan had only come to enlist his help in righting a terrible wrong.

Imagine the shock when the king of Israel heard the simple words, "You are the man!" David had been living in self-deception, covering his inner misery with an outward facade. Suddenly, Nathan had stripped back the veneer, exposing the sin and failure of the king's heart. Then Nathan went on to explain how God had given David so much, yet he had selfishly ignored God's commandments by committing murder and adultery.

Next, Nathan enumerated a series of life-shattering consequences David would experience. His household would be marked by tragedy, scandal, grief, and disgrace. The prophet's pronouncement proved to be unerringly true.

First, the infant son of David and Bathsheba died shortly after his birth. Later, the king's daughter Tamar was sexually assaulted and socially disgraced by her half-brother Amnon.

Then David's beloved son Absalom—blessed with luxuriously long hair, personal charm, and self-serving ambition—incited a rebellion which drove the king from his throne and his home in Jerusalem. To rub salt into the wound, Absalom humiliated his father even further by consorting publicly with the royal harem, an act of considerable political import in ancient Near Eastern society.

Following David's return to his throne, the king was forced to contend with yet another rebellion, followed by three years of famine and a plague that swept the kingdom.

Nathan, as a true friend, not only confronted David about his sin, but he also comforted the king with word of God's grace. First he affirmed God's forgiveness, telling David he would not die as a consequence of his sin, even though the king had given the enemies of God plenty of reason to mock God's name (2 Samuel 12:13–14). Then, after the baby born to David and Bathsheba died as the prophet predicted, Nathan returned with word that God would allow the next child born to this union to live. His name was *Jedidiah*, which means "beloved of the Lord." We know him better by his other given name— Solomon.

Following these events, Nathan continued a loyal friendship with David, Bathsheba, and their son Solomon. Years later when the king neared death and his eldest surviving son, Adonijah, threatened to seize the kingdom, it was Nathan who joined forces with Zadok the priest and two other men to diffuse the threat. Nathan himself came to Bathsheba, and the two of them developed and carried out a plan to warn the aging king that his desire to pass the kingdom on to Solomon was being threatened.

Lessons from a Prodigal King

Three lessons are evident as we examine "the prodigal fling of David the king." First, failure doesn't happen overnight. Typically, the seeds have been sown well in advance, perhaps over a period of years. They then manifest themselves in a careless attitude toward sin, the cultivation of ungoverned passions, an indifference toward discipline, a sense of personal entitlement, or just "going through the motions" when it comes to spiritual matters.

Serious illnesses like cancer seldom appear in the body without a background of previous symptoms. A massive and healthy looking tree suddenly falls in a thunderstorm, but an undetected decay in its trunk has been developing for years. In the same way, obvious visible failure by a Christian is generally preceded by an extended period of secret sin, of inward failure. That's why it is so important that we keep "short accounts" with the Lord, that we maintain discipline and integrity, and that we walk day by day with spiritually clean hands and pure hearts.

Second, the right kind of friendship and accountability can help keep us from sin. The New Testament urges us to encourage each other daily so that no one becomes hardened through sin's deceitfulness (Hebrews 3:13). Although he may have succeeded as David's military commander, Joab was a failure as David's friend. Nathan, on the other hand, showed the courage to confront the king over his failure, provided encouragement by reminding the king of God's gracious forgiveness, and then continued loyal to David over the years that followed. We all need Nathans in our lives, men and women who have the courage—and our permission—to hold us to accounts.

There's a final lesson from David's prodigal fling. No matter how terrible or how tragic a sin may be, two truths are always evident. First, God always offers forgiveness. Second, there will typically be consequences. God's grace wipes out the guilt and the stain of sin. As the psalmist himself expressed it, "As far as the east is from the west, so far has He removed our transgressions from us" (Psalm 103:12). The prophet Micah described God as casting our sins into the depths of the sea (Micah 7:19). Isaiah explained how God turns the scarlet color of our sins white as snow (Isaiah 1:18). Jeremiah spoke of God's choosing both to forgive and to forget our sins (Jeremiah 31:34).

Yet the scars of prodigal behavior frequently remain long after the sin is forgiven. Individuals who have engaged in sexual misconduct often suffer the lingering and even fatal consequences of sexually transmitted diseases. Broken marriages may never be restored, and devastated children may never fully recover from the effects of such betrayal.

The reality of sin's consequences is clearly illustrated by the story of the young boy who, whenever he misbehaved, was told to drive a nail into the back wall of the barn near his house. Whenever he sought and obtained forgiveness for a specific wrong, he was allowed to pull the nail out of the wall. One day with delight he told his dad, "I've taken care of all the wrongs I've done. I'm completely forgiven." His dad watched as he pulled the final nail out of the wall. Sadly, yet wisely, he then said to his dad, "But look how the nail holes have left the wall full of scars."

So it is with believers—God forgives prodigal behavior, but all too frequently the scars remain.

The Prayer of David

Have mercy upon me, O God,
    according to Your lovingkindness;
According to the multitude of your mercies,
    blot out my transgressions.
Wash me thoroughly from my iniquity,
    and cleanse me from my sin.
For I acknowledge my transgressions,
    and my sin is always before me.
Against You, You only, have I sinned,
    and done this evil in Your sight —
That You may be found just when You speak,
    and blameless when You judge.

—from Psalm 51

CHAPTER ELEVEN

Jonah: The Man Who Tried to Run from God

The remarkable thing about fearing God is that when you fear God you fear nothing else, whereas if you do not fear God you fear everything else.

—Oswald Chambers

Faith is not believing in spite of evidence but obeying in spite of consequences.

—Warren W. Wiersbe

Although his name meant "dove," Jonah was hawkish about God's punishment of those the prophet felt deserving of divine wrath. He grew up in Gath Hepher, a town in the territory of the tribe of Zebulun in ancient Palestine. Following the reigns of David and Solomon, his nation had divided into two separate countries, Israel in the north and Judah in the south. Jonah lived during the morally bankrupt reign of Jereboam II, the most powerful of all the northern kings. Jonah had predicted Israel's boundaries would be extended under his rule—a prediction which came true (2 Kings 14:25).

Yet Jonah was clearly aware of the imperfections of his country. Israel was a spiritually rebellious nation whose people had ignored the true God to worship idols. Another prophet, Amos, had also warned Israel against her stubbornness, suggesting that because of God's wrath the kingdom would likely be conquered by a Gentile nation from the east (Amos 5:27). This prediction was graphically fulfilled in 722 B.C. when Sargon II of Assyria conquered the nation.

Despite Israel's flaws, Jonah still loved his country and would do just about anything to postpone God's judgment. As he considered the threat of Assyria looming from the northeast, he concluded that's where God's judgment was likely to come from. After all, moral and spiritual degradation in Assyria was even greater than in Israel.

Even though they had declined temporarily during the reign of Jeroboam, the Assyrians were still a powerful nation. They are considered by Bible scholars to be one of history's cruelest nations. They frequently hung their enemies on stakes, skinned them, piled their bodies into large stacks, and burned them. Captives were often mutilated in hideous fashion. One captured leader was pierced through the chin with a dagger, tied with a rope, and forced to occupy a doghouse. The prophet Nahum referred to their capital, Nineveh, as the "City of Blood."

What a frightening thought for this prophet of God! Somehow the cruel nation of Assyria might become the source of God's judgment on His people Israel. Assyria's corruption, drunkenness, and self-indulgence were only exceeded by its cruel atrocities. Day after day Jonah may have prayed, "May Israel be saved, and may Nineveh be destroyed."

The Prodigal Prophet

One day God spoke to Jonah: "Arise; go to Nineveh, that great city, and cry out against it; for their wickedness has come up before Me." Jonah must have felt overwhelmed with confusion and mixed emotions.

First he might have thought, *Great! God is finally fed up with those pagans.* Then he may have paused in midthought. *But what if they repent? I doubt that would happen, but suppose it did. It would be terrible!* As he considered this he probably thought, *Repentance, that's what the Lord wants. He wants them to repent. But if they repent, God will probably use them to bring judgment on Israel, and my people will be destroyed.*

No way, Jonah thought. Not even God could make him conspire against his own country. So instead of heading for Nineveh, Jonah went the other way just as fast as he could. From the prophet's perspective, it was unthinkable that God cared about these pagan Gentiles. The concept of Israel as a missionary to the nations around her was just a little bit beyond the scope of Jonah's thinking.

If Jonah had been walking in fellowship and obedience with the Lord, he would have immediately set out for the northeast. Nineveh was located on the banks of the Tigris River, approximately 550 miles northeast of Samaria, the capital of the northern kingdom. It probably would have taken the prophet a month to reach the outskirts of Nineveh, then another three days to travel throughout the city. The second largest city in the world, smaller only than Babylon, Nineveh was also the oldest city in history, tracing its roots to Nimrod, the mighty hunter (Genesis 10:8–10). In addition to its atrocities, Nineveh was noted for its idolatry, including the worship of Ishtar, the goddess of love and war. Temples to several additional gods were located within the city.

Like many prodigals today, Jonah heard God's Word, then decided he had a better plan. The only prophet ever to run from God's commission, Jonah headed in the opposite direction from which he was told to go. He headed west to Jaffa, where he boarded a ship which was bound for Tarshish, a Phoenician seaport and smelting operation in southern Spain, some 2,500 miles west. Apparently, Jonah had the idea he could actually get away from God's presence by heading to Tarshish.

Nothing could be further from the truth.

As the Bible says in the Psalms, there is simply no place we can go where God isn't present. Although Jonah may have wanted to resign from being God's prophet and avoid God's assignment, he could never get away from the presence of the Lord (Psalm 139:7–10).

Billy had been called to preach. He knew it from the time he had trusted Christ as his Savior at a summer camp at the age of eleven. Initially he had been excited about preaching God's Word, especially as he spent time reading the Bible every day and faithfully attending a Bible-teaching church.

Then, when he was fifteen, Billy's parents divorced. Angry at God for not keeping his mom and dad together, the teenager dropped out of church and began hanging out with a crowd that had no use for spiritual things. His unkempt, shoulder-length hair, his large earrings, his participation in shoplifting forays, his habit of smoking almost a pack of cigarettes a day and getting "tanked" on cheap beer every weekend—all were outward symbols of an inwardly seething heart in rebellion against the God who had called Billy to serve Him but who, Billy felt, had let him down.

In Billy's life, like Jonah's, the real issue was "who's in charge of the universe?" Neither liked the way God had been running things. Jonah may have tried to put such feelings aside as he climbed into the ship and fell asleep. After all, better to sleep than to face the pain of life, especially when it comes from rebellion against the loving Creator.

The Price of Rebellion

Jonah paid a high price for his rebellion. The cost of the fare for the three-year journey to Tarshish must have been very expensive, and there were no refunds—just as in the case of the prodigal son. And in Jonah's life, just as in the prodigal's, God never lets him get away with it.

While the prophet slept in the hold of the ship, a massive storm came up quickly. It was so severe that the ship nearly broke up. The Phoenician sailors cried out to their various gods as they began pitching their cargo into the sea in an attempt to keep the ship from sinking.

Jonah, physically exhausted and spiritually desensitized, continued to sleep. He had understood and rejected God's mission. In the past, he had served in the school of the prophets and successfully proclaimed God's message in those days, but now he had deliberately chosen to disobey God. Perhaps the ease with which he had been able to secure a ticket on the trip allowed him to rationalize his behavior: *Maybe God had changed His mind, and this trip was really God's will.* Instead, Jonah sailed right into a storm.

The prophet's sleep was rudely interrupted by the captain's urgent cry. "Call on your God!" the sailor yelled above the noise of the waves and storm. "Maybe He will hear us and keep us from being killed."

This shipmaster must have been a man of some experience. He recognized that this was not your common, garden-variety storm. From his idolatrous background, he must have decided this was the judgment of a god, so he figured someone on board must be the cause. Collecting all the men, he ordered them to cast lots. "It's time we find out who's to blame."

Not surprisingly, the lot fell on Jonah. The storm was indeed a judgment. It wasn't an act of revenge on the part of God, but the Lord's loving, gracious discipline. One thing is clear from the Bible: a caring father always disciplines his prodigal children. Such discipline is an evidence of His love and is to be endured rather than avoided.

Both of us had fathers who loved us. We know they loved us because they disciplined us. They weren't abusive about it. They were fair and loving. They were also extremely firm. Both Frank Kroll and Jim Hawkins believed in appropriate corporal punishment. Neither of us liked it at the time, but we both endured it. Later we came to see its value in increasing measure as we grew up and became involved in serving the Lord.

Storm of Discipline

Jonah must have come to recognize that the storm was an act of God's discipline as the Phoenician sailors peppered him with questions.

"For whose cause has this trouble come upon us?"

"Mine," Jonah replied.

"What's your occupation, your business?"

"I'm a prophet of God." Maybe he didn't tell them immediately, but eventually he admitted he had quit his job as a prophet and was trying to run from God's presence.

"Where did you come from?"

"From the land of the Hebrews where I serve Yahweh, the God of heaven, who made the sea and the dry land."

Immediately, the men got the point. "The Creator of heaven and earth, and you think you can escape from Him? That's total insanity! Why have you done this?" they asked anxiously.

After they had questioned Jonah at length and as the storm persisted, the men realized they needed to do something to save their lives. They asked Jonah what they had to do to stop the storm. Jonah replied by suggesting that they pick him up and throw him into the sea. Perhaps the prophet wasn't even thinking about God's direction, but apparently God had permitted this since He planned to use Jonah's experience for His own glory.

At first the sailors refused. Unwilling to drown the servant of such a powerful God who controlled the elements, they decided instead to try saving his life and theirs. But as the sea continued raging, they finally gave up and followed the prophet's advice. First, they did something they had never done before. They cried out to Jonah's God, the true God. It was a remarkable contrast to their first efforts at prayer when each had cried out to his own god. They acknowledged God's sovereignty and prayed that the Lord would spare their lives. Then they tossed Jonah into the sea. Instantly the incredible storm ceased.

It was a powerful testimony to the sovereign power of God. He could use even a rebellious prodigal prophet to cause this group of pagans to glorify His name.

There are two lessons from Jonah's experience that have implications for us. First, God is capable of using even individuals who are living in rebellion and are sinning against Him.

Second, He is far more pleased when we obey Him, when our lives are morally clean, and we serve Him in respectful trust.

Charlie learned both these lessons the hard way. When he went off to college, he chose to leave behind the Christian convictions he had developed while growing up in a pastor's home, choosing instead the fraternity-driven lifestyle of a party animal. "I can best serve God by hanging out with my fraternity brothers, partying along with them, proving to them that Christians can have a good time the same way they do," he rationalized.

"I'll never forget how it hit home at a party one night," he related, "and one of my fraternity buddies said, 'Charlie, I don't understand it—you tell me you're a Christian, but you get drunk and chase girls right along with the rest of us. It just doesn't compute.' When I woke up stone cold sober the next morning, it was like his words were on a tape playing over and over in my mind. God used that to remind me that He wanted to clean up my life. I had lost my high school sweetheart, the respect of my family, and most important of all, the joy of walking closely with the Lord the way I had experienced all through high school."

After the storm ended, the sailors, new converts to the true God, expressed their fear and faith by offering a sacrifice to Him and making vows. As this happened on board ship, the prodigal prophet sank below the waves.

A Great Fish

The story of "Jonah and the Whale" has become as familiar to Sunday school alumni as that of David and Goliath. However, this massive sea creature is not specifically called a whale but "a great fish."

This great sea creature could very well have been a sperm whale which can swallow even a fifteen-foot shark. Another possibility is the whale shark, otherwise known as *rhinedon typicus*, which has been known to swallow men who were later found alive in the shark's stomach.[1] Dr. Harry Rimmer, who was president of the Research Science Bureau of Los Angeles, described several cases in which persons were swallowed by large fish and survived. Dr. Rimmer writes of a personal encounter in 1926 with a man who was swallowed by a white shark and survived. He noted the striking physical appearance of the survivor, his body completely void of hair, and with patches of skin that appeared bleached, apparently due to the effect of digestive juices.[2]

Few places could be as miserable as the stomach of a fish. Imagine the disgusting mix of semi-digested food and caustic gastric juices! To get a taste of how bad it must have been, go down to the dock in some seaport where professional fishermen are cleaning their catch. The nauseous odor you'll encounter probably doesn't even begin to compare with Jonah's experience.

Jonah's major concern at this point wasn't his appearance. He undoubtedly expected to die. Perhaps he preferred death to repentance. Yet his sovereign God knew what was best for Jonah. The fish swallowed him whole, and he remained there for three days. Miraculously, he was somehow able to breathe. Incredibly, he was not digested. Supernaturally, God permitted him to keep his senses so he could pray from the depths of the fish. In the first chapter of Jonah's book the prodigal prophet refused to pray, although later the pagans prayed three times. Finally, in the depths of this fish Jonah prayed. Later the prophet would commit his prayer to writing. Like the prodigal in the pigpen, Jonah's prayer was short and to the point.

First, he repented. When he first received God's commission, his mind was made up. Like concrete it was thoroughly set, and from his perspective impossible to change.

Yet the Creator God was capable of arranging circumstances in such a way so that even the mind of this stubborn prophet would change. In a compactly crafted poem, Jonah described how he cried to God from the belly of the grave, how he considered himself dead, but how God had reinstated his life. He appealed to God and God heard him.

That's how it is when we change our mind about our prodigal behavior and cry out to God. He is always there. He never forgets us. He only wants us to remember Him (Jonah 2:7).

Having remembered the Lord, Jonah promised to offer the sacrifice God wanted from his life—to pay the vow he had made when he became a prophet. Then he acknowledged, "Salvation is of the Lord."

At that point God prompted the fish to spew the prophet out so that he wound up on dry ground. Jonah was not injured, but it's likely his physical appearance had been drastically changed—his hair removed and his skin discolored by the digestive juices of the fish. One thing is certain: his heart had been changed from within. No, he hadn't dealt with all his prodigal issues yet, but he learned the lesson that God, not Jonah, was in charge of the universe. He undoubtedly returned to Jerusalem to give thanks, hoping God would be satisfied with the punishment he had endured and the repentance he had chosen.

Surely God wouldn't call him to Nineveh again.

But He did.

The book of Jonah is a book of superlatives. Nineveh is referred to as a *great* city, and the storm was a *great* storm. Jonah was swallowed by a *great* fish. Jonah's own emotions ranged from *great* displeasure to *great* happiness. Furthermore, God worked a *great* miracle to give Jonah another opportunity to respond, but He didn't change the prophet's responsibility.

A Second Chance

Before long God called out to Jonah a second time. The message was identical to the first, and it clearly illustrated an important truth: God is the God of the Second Chance. In fact, He delights in extending multiple chances, but He also expects us to respond to the new opportunity He is giving us at any one time. In His new directive to Jonah, God reminded him that he still must travel to Nineveh and preach the message God had given him.

Apparently three days spent in the belly of the fish was sufficient to persuade Jonah of the value of obeying God. Still the prophet continued to struggle, for God didn't tell Jonah to "Tell these people what's on your heart." Rather, the Lord wanted Jonah to preach what was on His heart. His message was one of sin, judgment, and a call to repentance.

Apparently the prophet was to spend three days working his way through the city, preaching across a metropolitan area that extended for some twenty miles up and down the Tigris River. Archeological excavations have indicated the wall of the city and its suburbs was sixty miles around and one hundred feet high, with numerous defensive towers ringing the city. The total circumference of Nineveh was about sixty miles.

So Jonah obeyed the Lord God, entered Nineveh, and preached to its depraved inhabitants. He must have been convinced that the people of Nineveh would think he was crazy. As cruel as they were, they'd probably skin him alive and put him on a stick. Perhaps he was scared to death, but he began walking through the city, crying out just one shocking statement, "Yet forty days, and Nineveh shall be overthrown."

God was extending His grace to the Ninevites and giving them an opportunity to avoid divine judgment by repenting, just as He did Jonah. For three days the prophet moved through the city before reaching the eastern edge (Jonah 4:5).

A Repentant Response

Word spread rapidly throughout the city. Incredibly, people listened—and they responded by repenting. As evidence of their belief in God, the king of Nineveh proclaimed a fast, and both he and the people put on sackcloth and sat in ashes, the common Near Eastern sign of grief and humiliation. It must have been an incredible sight to see these ferocious, debauched people humbled in repentance, seeking to turn away God's hand of judgment. What could account for this dramatic response to Jonah's preaching?

According to Luke's gospel, the Lord Jesus described Jonah himself as a sign (perhaps because of his appearance) in addition to the message he preached (Luke 11:30–32). Ironically, one of the gods worshipped by the Assyrians was Dagon who was represented by an image half man and half fish. Perhaps seeing the physical effects of being swallowed by the fish and hearing the story of deliverance by the God of the universe prompted them to repent. Jonah's body bore the marks of repentance, but his message gave the encouraging word of a second chance. The Assyrians of Nineveh, proud and cruel, believed Jonah's God and repented of their sin, thinking "perhaps God will be gracious to us as well."

Authentic repentance always begins as a change of mind from arrogant self-will to humble submission. Ultimately, it leads to a change of life. That's what happened in Jonah's case, and it's precisely the response we see in the lives of the Assyrians. For the fifth time in this brief book, prayer takes place. God answered their prayer, saw their works, and graciously withheld judgment.

It's important to understand that God didn't repent or change His mind in the way we change ours. Rather, what we see in Jonah 3:10 is a change in God's decree, based on a condition and a response. Had there been no repentance, Nineveh would have been overthrown—the word Jonah used was the same term used by Moses to describe the overthrow of the city of Sodom by fire. Yet the response of the Ninevites and the gracious act of God demonstrated the truth originally recorded by the prophet Ezekiel, " 'Do I have any pleasure at all that the wicked should die?' says the Lord God, 'and not that he should turn from his ways and live?' " (Ezekiel 18:23). As the New Testament also observes, "God resists the proud, but gives grace to the humble" (James 4:6).

Jonah's Heart

Jonah must have watched the response of these people with a sinking heart. The people of Nineveh didn't have a clue as to what God was like. They were a violent people, so they must have figured God was violent and vindictive too. Jonah was aware of God's great loyal love. He knew they could expect to be forgiven if they repented. Maybe he hadn't bothered to tell them that.

So God had chosen not to overthrow the city in the way Jonah had expected. Even though such cataclysmic judgment didn't occur, Nineveh was nonetheless overthrown, for the people's lives had drastically changed. Where once they had practiced dishonesty, corruption, cruelty, drunkenness, and shameful pleasure, now they cried out in grief to God, sat in sackcloth and ashes, fasted, prayed, and mourned. The old Nineveh was overthrown, gone forever. Out of the ashes of repentance rose a new Nineveh, a Nineveh of people who had submitted their proud wills and shameful ways to the one true and holy God.

Yet Jonah the prophet was heartbroken. What a shocking response to see the prophet seated outside the city, extremely displeased and doing a slow but intense burn.

An entire prodigal nation had turned to God! Surely any prophet worth his salt would be filled with joy! Yet the book of Jonah has some of the strangest twists of any book in the Bible. It is evident that the prophet had an incredulous attitude as he saw these people who once took great joy in torturing others transformed into God's humble servants.

So what was going on in Jonah's heart?

First and foremost, he was self-willed. In effect, he was saying, "God, I told you so. I warned you these people would repent. I knew you were gracious, and that's why I ran away in the first place. God, I just didn't approve of your plan—and I still don't."

There were two reasons Jonah felt this way. One had to do with his patriotism toward Israel, for now this precipitated an even greater risk of God using the Assyrians to punish His people.

Second, and perhaps more to the point, was the embarrassment, the personal humiliation for Jonah. Now his prophetic reputation had been damaged, perhaps beyond repair in his estimation.

God's immediate response to the prophet's question was to grab his attention, to seek his repentance by forcing him to think about his emotions. The Lord must have wanted Jonah to see that while the Ninevites had moved *toward* God's merciful heart, Jonah had moved *away*. In his anger the prophet admitted that he wanted to see God "smoke" Nineveh. There was a grudge in his heart toward the Assyrians and bitterness toward the Lord Himself.

Bitter Toward God

During his prodigal years after his parents divorced, Billy, too, struggled with that kind of bitterness. Then one day, after a tragic accident in which Billy was seriously injured and two friends were killed—an accident caused by Billy's drunken condition—he genuinely repented and turned his life over to the Lord, promising to let God do with him as He wished. He attended Bible college, then seminary, and later entered the ministry.

Yet for years Billy continued to struggle. His was a harsh, legalistic ministry, one that seldom reflected the grace of God and that seemed to always hammer at people rather than uplift them.

Years later, following a series of medical problems in his life, Billy finally came to the understand his own negative spirit. Bitterness toward God over the divorce of his parents had produced a root that had bitterly flavored not only his prodigal behavior but his subsequent ministry as well. Like Jonah, Billy needed to face God's question, "Is it right for you to be angry? Do you do well to harbor bitterness?"

Jonah's answer to God's initial question was not recorded. Perhaps the prophet didn't respond at all. But his actions certainly made his attitude clear. Leaving the city, he went out to the eastern side and built a crude hut for himself so he could sit in the shade and watch. It's not difficult to guess what must have been going on in the prophet's mind. *Yes, God may have given the city a reprieve, but maybe they'll still do something to anger Him. After all, the forty days haven't passed yet. These people have been so incredibly wicked. Would God actually hold back the judgment they deserve just because of a repentance that can only be measured in days? What about all those past years of cruelty and shame?*

What we see here is a prophet who still preferred to be a prodigal, who still wanted to see God do things Jonah's way rather than God's way.

In response, God lovingly prepared several object lessons to help the prophet get in touch with what was wrong about his emotions. There were lessons to be learned by this prodigal prophet, and God was capable of arranging just the circumstances to teach him. First, a luxuriant vine or plant grew suddenly. Its foliage provided cover, shading Jonah from the blazing sun.

This must be a sign from God, he may have thought. *He must want me to stay here. Perhaps He's going to let me see what I've wanted to see all the time—the destruction of this city by fire. Now He's provided me with a comfortable observation booth.*

But the prophet's thinking changed drastically the next morning when he discovered the plant's leaves withered. When Jonah inspected the plant, he discovered a worm—again prepared by God—which had damaged the plant so that it withered. Once again the prophet was at the mercy of the burning sun. Then God sent a scorching east wind to intensify the already intolerable heat.

Jonah's pleasure quickly turned to angry grief as his hopes, so recently revived, were now shattered. There wasn't a chance God would destroy the Ninevites—they would only be used to punish his own people. Again Jonah voiced the depths of his feelings. At the point of passing out, ready to give up, he expressed a suicidal depression. "I wish I were dead. It's better for me to die than to live."

Yet the God who caused the large plant to cover his booth, directed the worm to the plant, and finally sent the scorching east wind wasn't through working on the prophet. After all, He was the same God who had earlier sent the storm and the fish.

A Question Repeated

Again God asked Jonah the question with which He had confronted the prophet earlier, "Do you have a right to be angry?" This time God added a question about the vine.

There was a clear-cut message for Jonah in all this, one that though it seems almost unthinkable, the prophet very nearly missed. Jonah's attitude—his preoccupation with himself, his agenda, and his own comfort—had caused him to despise what was valuable while he loved what was worthless.

The problem at the heart of Jonah's struggle was that he still didn't understand who was in charge of the universe. His root problem was the root problem of every prodigal. Who is really in charge?

Jonah had not caused the Assyrians to become a nation in the first place, nor had he drawn them to repentance. He had not caused the vine to grow up, nor had he brought about its demise. Clearly, Jonah had more concern for a large weed than a human life. This prophet of God was more worried over his personal comfort and welfare than with the spiritual and even physical welfare of hundreds of thousands of people.

Jonah never spent any time cultivating the plant. All he had done was enjoy its benefits. The city of Nineveh, with its people and its animals, were part of God's creation, loved by the Creator who had sought their repentance even when they were at the outer limits of rebellion.

"Elder Brother" Prophet

Just like the elder brother, Jonah had been quick to dish out the harshness of God's judgment without the balance of God's love and mercy. He was eager to protest in order to protect his own interests, while he showed a callous lack of regard for the needs of others. Curiously, when God asked the second time, "Is it right for you to be angry about the plant?" Jonah furiously responded, "It is right for me to be angry, even to death."

Graciously, the Lord pointed out through the example of the plant how He had taken pity toward those who were spiritually blind, helpless, and ignorant of God's standards. Jonah, by contrast, had shown himself to be plagued by the same selfish, blind unrighteousness of the elder brother and of the Pharisees of Jesus' day.

It is important to understand that God wasn't condemning Jonah's passionate concern for his own country. Nor was He rebuking Jonah for hating the sins of Israel's enemy. Jonah hadn't learned to draw the distinction between sin and the sinner.

It was a distinction Billy hadn't learned in his early ministry as time after time he found himself angrily driving away the very people God wanted to reach out to. In fact, during a stint as the pastor of a church located near a university, he told his church board, "I'd just as soon those young rebels not come here. They're not going to repent anyway. They're smelly, long-haired, and rebellious, and I don't care for the kind of music they like either."

At heart, Billy—like Jonah—was trying to tell God how to run the universe and how to deal with people. So many times our anger toward others may really mask our desire for control. This angry prophet demonstrated an insensitive disregard for other people, mingled with a subtle yet clear desire to take some measure of the control that rightly belongs to the Creator alone.

Like a spiritual cancer, Jonah's callous disregard for both God and people ate away at the joy that could have been his had he not persisted in his prodigal behavior. We cannot measure his prodigal experience in terms of days of agony in the belly of the fish or hours of torture under a burning sun. No, the ultimate misery experienced by Jonah was brought on by his personal rebellion against the will of God.

Yet his story has a happy ending. Ultimately, Jonah must have submitted to his heavenly Father. We can assume this because Jonah wrote the book. It is a book whose conclusion seems to leave matters dangling. Yet in the abruptness of its ending, it seems apparent that Jonah finally realized who was in control. Finally he must have learned the lesson Jesus taught as life priorities: we are to submit to God in wholehearted love and to love others unconditionally. It certainly took a long time, but that seems to be the lesson Jonah finally learned.

And what are the lessons we can learn from the life of this prodigal prophet? One is that we need to remove the log that blocks our own vision before attempting to pull a splinter from someone else's eye (see Matthew 7:1–5). It is easy for us to become blinded by our self-righteous anger toward certain classes of sinners. We may desire so strongly for God to punish them that we not only fail to act lovingly or even decently toward them but we also refuse to recognize our own sinfulness and failure.

Barry considered himself one of the most militant Christians in his church. He had debated a secular humanist, demonstrated against homosexuals, and picketed abortion clinics. He angrily confronted the young women who came to the clinics, accusing them of sins ranging from promiscuity to murder.

Yet it wasn't until Barry's girlfriend, Sheila, told him she was pregnant that he was forced to come to grips with his own sinful heart and actions. Finally, with tears in his eyes he confessed to his pastor, "I was the hypocrite who needed to cast the beam out of my own eye before I could help my brother get the speck out of his eye" (see Matthew 7:5).

So one important lesson we can learn from Jonah is to beware of hypocrisy, to be careful of condemning others without examining our hearts, attitudes, and actions.

A second lesson is that our hatred of sin must be tempered by love for sinners. The best approach to those caught in the consequences of immoral or unbiblical lifestyles is to offer the open hand of compassion and provide practical alternatives rather than pointing a finger of accusation.

It's easy for us to consider ourselves immune to the weaknesses that are so easy to spot in others and to develop an insensitivity to our own areas of failure. May God give us the sensitivity to deal with the sin in our own lives and a compassion for others who fail.

Endnotes

1. John D. Hannah, "Jonah," *Bible Knowledge Commentary* (Chicago: Victor Books, 1985), 1:1463.

2. Madison Leslie, *An Exposition of the Book of Jonah* (St. Louis: Miracle Press, 1973), 367.

CHAPTER TWELVE

Miriam:
The Green-Eyed Prodigal

O! Beware, my lord, of jealousy; It is the green-ey'd monster which doth mock the meat it feeds on.

—Shakespeare, *Othello*

She became one of the most prominent women in the Old Testament, occupying an important leadership role in Israel during and after the Exodus. For decades, she commanded great respect from the Israelites as she wrote and led in corporate songs of praise to the Lord God.

Yet, like many others, Miriam failed to finish well. Her struggle with jealousy is one any of us who have battled the green-eyed monster can relate to. The terrible consequences she experienced and the ultimate disgrace of leprosy she endured show the serious nature of her particular kind of prodigal behavior. Sadly, Miriam was old enough to know better when it happened.

So are many of us who allow the seeds of envy and discontent to take root and blossom, often with tragic consequence.

A Notable Beginning

Miriam was born in a godly home in Goshen, the part of Egypt where the Israelites lived and worked as slaves. Her parents, Amram and Jochebed, were of the tribe of Levi, later the priestly tribe of Israel. The Bible indicates they were a godly couple, people of faith, even though they lived in a time of intense struggle and conflict.

Rigorous slave labor failed to prevent the population of Israelites from growing. Afraid of being outnumbered by a foreign people, the Egyptian pharaoh commanded the midwives who served the Hebrew people to put every male child to death. Because of their faith in God, however, the Hebrew midwives refused (Exodus 1:15). Since their actions guarded the sanctity of human life, God blessed these midwives and gave them homes and families of their own.

Against this grim backdrop of attempted ethnic cleansing, the book of Exodus describes the birth of "a son . . . a beautiful child" (Exodus 2:2). Aaron and Miriam, the two older children in the home, must have felt a measure of excitement about the birth of a new baby, and when they discovered they had a younger brother, it must have been a thrill for the entire family.

For three months the family, keenly aware of Pharaoh's edict that every Hebrew boy child be killed, worked to hide the existence of the infant. Finally, Jochebed realized that her infant could no longer be hidden. Her baby was no ordinary child, and their faith in Jehovah far outweighed any fear of the king's edict. So she enlisted her daughter, Miriam, in a plan to save the boy's life.

Baby in a Basket

Constructing a woven basket from papyrus reeds taken from the marshes near the river, Jochebed waterproofed it by coating the basket with tar. Then she carefully placed the baby in it and slipped the basket into the dense reeds where the waters of the Nile lapped against the shore.

In a sense Jochebed was fulfilling the edict of Pharaoh Amenhotep—to drown the male Israelite babies in the Nile—as she placed the basket with the baby inside into the waters of the river.

Sister Miriam had been enlisted by her mother to stand nearby and wait to see what would happen. The presence of a little girl playing along the shoreline would probably not arouse the suspicion of the Egyptians. Although Miriam may have pretended to play, her attention was undoubtedly focused on her little brother and the basket.

Suddenly Miriam heard voices approaching. It was the daughter of Pharaoh with her retinue of attendants, coming to the river to bathe. Spotting the little basket floating among the reeds at the edge of the river, the crown princess ordered one of her maids to bring it to her. When she opened the basket, she discovered the baby, who immediately started crying. This moved the princess with compassion, even though she realized that this was one of the Hebrew males her father had ordered killed.

With a courage and a sense of poise beyond her years, young Miriam stepped forward and volunteered to seek a nurse from among the Hebrew women. The Egyptian princess agreed, and Miriam, undoubtedly following her mother's plan carefully, brought Jochebed herself to serve as nurse. In doing so, young Miriam helped save her brother's life and became a key tool in the sovereign hand of the God who had important plans for all three of Amram and Jochebed's children.

Thus, at an early age Miriam demonstrated the kind of woman she would become. She obeyed her mother who had crafted the plan, which was apparently designed to take advantage of the princess' bathing schedule and her compassionate response to finding an abandoned infant. The baby was named Moses—the name means "drawn out," an appropriate description of how he had been taken from the deadly waters of the Nile. He would be raised as the son of Pharaoh's daughter and given the advantages of the extensive education available in Pharaoh's court.

It isn't difficult to see the sovereign hand of God guiding events in Miriam's family. The same thing could be seen in the modern-day experience of Julie. Born to a single mother, growing up on the mean streets of the south side of Chicago, Julie could have gotten into trouble with the law at an early age—or worse. However, God brought Elizabeth and Gerry, who were involved in a ministry to young people in the Chicago housing projects, into Julie's life. They reached out to her in love and shared the reality of Christ with her. Julie came to faith at an early age, then began growing in the Lord. Unlike many of her contemporaries who became unwed mothers, drug addicts, or even criminals, Julie decided to allow her life to be used for the Lord's glory. She attended Bible college, and then became a career missionary.

Seeing God's Work

Eighty years elapsed before Miriam's story continues in the biblical record. Apparently she never married, and the focus of her life was loving and serving God and His people. She had witnessed the indignities inflicted on her fellow Israelites by the vicious taskmasters of Egypt and shared her people's fear, sorrows, and pain. As she witnessed the cruelty and the beatings, she must have encouraged her fellow Israelites and lifted her voice along with theirs in steadfast prayer to God for deliverance. Hers was a ministry of hope and encouragement in the face of incredible adversity, urging her compatriots to keep their faith in God alive. There was still hope of deliverance even though that hope must have diminished somewhat as year after difficult year passed.

For forty long years Moses had been gone from Egypt, sought by the authorities because of the death of an Egyptian. Miriam must have known in her heart that one day he would return. While every passing year must have made it harder to wait, she still waited, still hoped, still trusted.

Finally the day came when the brother she had loved as a baby returned, a robust, mature man of eighty. Like her older brother, Aaron, Miriam stayed by Moses' side to encourage and support him through his struggles. As he repeatedly confronted Pharaoh, she was convinced that God had chosen her brother to set their people free, and the miracles God performed at Moses' hand confirmed that conviction. She was privileged to witness the ten dreadful plagues God brought on Egypt at the hand of Moses and their devastating consequences.

As she saw God's supernatural power, she may have thought back to the miraculous way in which God had spared Moses as an infant and the role she had been privileged to play at that time.

Victory Celebration

Then came the day, following the first Passover supper, when God
told Moses and Aaron to lead the Israelites out of Egypt. Six hundred
thousand male heads of households, plus the rest of the families with
their flocks and herds, headed from Ramses to Succoth. God led the
Israelites with a massive cloud by day and a column of fire by night as
they traveled the way of the wilderness toward the sea (Exodus 13:18–
38).

In a short time, however, a paralyzing fear shot through the camp
of the Israelites when they discovered the Egyptian army in hot pursuit.
The Israelites appeared trapped between the sea of reeds and the
approaching army. They complained bitterly against Moses, accusing
him of deceiving them and dooming them to death in the desert.

Miriam watched as her brother refused to bow to the people's fury.
Calmly he instructed them, "Don't be afraid. Don't panic. Stand still.
Wait on the Lord. Watch for His deliverance. Keep silent. Don't
complain."

Then at God's instruction, Moses stretched out his staff, the waters
rolled back on either side, and Miriam, Aaron, and the people of Israel
walked across the dry seabed!

When they reached the other side of the sea, Miriam watched
anxiously as the chariots and horsemen of the mightiest military force
on earth pursued them along the dry path through the sea. She must
have felt exuberant relief as Moses again held out his rod and the
waters closed in, destroying the feared Egyptians and their horses and
chariots.

Their faith confirmed and their fears relieved, the Israelites joined
their leader in a great song of praise to the Lord for this amazing
miraculous victory. The Israelites sang,

> Who is like You, O LORD, among the gods?
> Who is like You, glorious in holiness,
> Fearful in praises, doing wonders?
> You stretched out Your right hand;
> The earth swallowed them.
> You in Your mercy have led forth
> The people whom You have redeemed;
> You have guided them in Your strength
> To Your holy habitation.
> —Exodus 15:11–13

In response to the song of praise written by her brother Moses, Miriam the prophetess—the first woman so designated in Scripture—took a tambourine and, although well into her nineties, led the women of Israel in a dance of praise with words still sung in praise today.

Sing to the LORD, for He has triumphed gloriously!
The horse and its rider He has thrown into the sea!
—Exodus 15:21

This brief passage, recorded by Moses in the Pentateuch, gives us an important clue as to the kind of person Miriam was. Though she was in her ninth decade of life, she was filled with energy, radiant in praise, ecstatic with joy—a positive force for leadership, just as Moses and his brother, Aaron, were among the men. Her designation as a prophetess demonstrated that she wasn't just a servant of Moses but had been recognized as a leader in her own right.

Strength to Weakness

Eventually Miriam's personal strength and leadership abilities led to feelings of bitterness and envy toward her brother Moses. Throughout Israel's wilderness journey, Miriam must have heard the people griping and complaining many times. It almost seemed like griping was the national pastime in Israel! Just as allergy symptoms inflict misery on large numbers of people today, the presence of griping and murmuring in Israel seemed to break out in full-blown epidemics. One such instance occurred in Exodus 15–17, immediately following the great victory celebrated by Miriam and Moses in song and dance. Another happened during a period of difficulty and defeat, following the incident with the golden calf at Mount Sinai and the refusal of the Israelites to claim the Promised Land at Kadesh Barnea (Numbers 14:16).

Griping, or murmuring, is speaking negatively against those in authority—human leaders like Moses or Aaron (Exodus 16:2; Numbers 14:2, 36) and ultimately against God Himself (Exodus 16:7–8; Numbers 14:27–29). Frequently, it results from unmet needs or expectations, such as the lack of food or water (Exodus 15:24; 16:2–3). The Hebrew word *lun* (found only in the Exodus and Numbers passages and in Joshua 9:18) signifies verbalized discontent, usually muted but audible, directed toward human leaders yet ultimately focused toward God Himself. It evidences a lack of faith and a rebellious refusal to obey. Just as fever demonstrates the presence of infection, murmuring, griping, or complaining indicate the presence of bitterness. Murmuring constituted a serious problem in the nation of Israel, one that God dealt with severely. The antidote for murmuring was to trust God and obey Him rather than to gripe or complain.

Miriam's strength in leadership, mixed with the bitterness she seemed to absorb from the people around her, led to an incident in which she chose to follow a prodigal path. As many have often pointed out, a strength when taken to an extreme can constitute a serious weakness.

The Israelites were leaving Mount Sinai, the scene of Moses' greatest moment of exaltation. The climate in the camp was one of both bitterness and jealousy. The Lord had instructed Moses to appoint seventy men as elders in Israel. They would be given a measure of the Spirit of God which was on Moses himself to empower them to help bear the burden of leadership (Numbers 11:16–17).

Shortly thereafter, two men, named Eldad and Medad, who had not been designated as elders, prophesied—evidence that they too had been empowered by the Spirit of God. Joshua, Moses' second in command, reacted sharply, suggesting that Moses forbid them from speaking. Moses' reply was to ask Joshua, "Are you zealous for my sake?" Clearly the camp's atmosphere was infected with murmuring, bitterness, and envy.

Moses' response to Joshua clearly indicated an attitude of grace and an absence of any envy as he expressed the wish that all the Lord's people would become prophets, filled with His Spirit (Numbers 11:29).

Confrontation at Hazeroth

A short time after this incident, the Israelites camped at a place called Hazeroth. Here Miriam, accompanied by her brother Aaron (who seemed to have a talent for following those who led in the wrong direction), criticized Moses because of his marriage to a Cushite woman.

This unexpected confrontation was apparently prompted by Miriam since the Hebrew language uses a feminine verb, indicating her leadership in this move against her brother. It must have hurt Moses deeply—if you've ever experienced an attack you didn't expect from someone you trusted, loved, and served with, you can understand in some measure what Moses must have felt.

The outward issue Miriam addressed was Moses' marriage to a woman from a foreign nation. Miriam claimed that such a marriage was completely unsuitable. Even though she had been something of a "surrogate mother" as well as a big sister to Moses many decades before, that time had long passed. And although she may have found his interracial marriage distasteful, there is nothing in the Bible to indicate that there was anything wrong with this marriage since the people of Cush were not on the list of idolatrous nations from whom the Israelites were not to marry (Exodus 34:11, 16).

The real issue was not Moses' marriage but his prominence in leadership. This is clear from the statement, "Has the Lord indeed spoken only through Moses? Has He not spoken through us also?" (Numbers 12:2). As is so often the case, a surface problem simply masked the heart of the matter. The real problem here was jealousy, which often grows in the fertile soil of bitterness (see James 3:14).

God had appointed Moses, Aaron, and Miriam to their leadership roles in the nation. Moses was the law-giver, what we might called the CEO today. Aaron served as high priest, and Miriam as prophetess and leader of the women. Undoubtedly the three had served for years as a team, confiding in each other, depending on each other, encouraging each other. Perhaps since Moses had remarried (Numbers 12:1), Miriam had begun to feel that she was being replaced by a new "first lady." Maybe her pride was wounded, and like termites eating into a wooden beam, envious feelings began to gnaw into her spirit. Soon a core of jealousy became evident as the woman who had led the women of Israel, supported her brother, and lifted up the name of God engaged in a petty game of envious carping. She challenged her brother's leadership role, ostensibly over his marriage, but the envious feelings had probably been present for years, eating away beneath the surface. Now they surfaced, evident for everyone to see.

Envy in the Camp

Within a year after Vince and his wife, Laura, founded a Christian camp on a picturesque lakeshore, Vince's older sister, Maxine, joined their ministry. Hard-working and never married, Maxine made the camp and Vince's ministry the focus of her life. On more than one occasion, Vince told public and private audiences he didn't know what he'd do without Maxine's administrative and secretarial skills.

Two years after Laura's tragic death from cancer, Vince remarried. Hazel, his new wife, was also a skilled administrator and secretary and had even stronger personal skills than Maxine. Before long, Vince and other members of his ministry team noticed Maxine beginning to do subtle things to undermine Hazel's role in the camp office, in the kitchen, and even in working with volunteers. As Vince lamented, "I just couldn't believe anyone of her maturity, experience, and service to the Lord would become so consumed with envy. But she sure was!"

The envy on the part of Miriam and Aaron was not prompted by any arrogance in Moses. The Bible makes this clear by the parenthetical statement, "Now the man Moses was very humble, more than all men who were on the face of the earth" (Numbers 12:3). As is usually the case, the real issue had little or nothing to do with the person against whom the envy was directed. Rather, it represented a spiritual failure, an internal prodigal choice on the part of the "green-eyed" individual.

Green-Eyed Monster

The Bible makes no bones about the destructive nature of envy. As Solomon put it, "A sound heart is life to the body, but envy is rottenness to the bones" (Proverbs 14:30). The book of Job describes envy, like anger, as a killer (Job 5:2). Solomon indicated that jealousy could be even more devastating than wrath or anger (Proverbs 27:4). Both David and Solomon warned against envying the seeming prosperity of the wicked (Psalm 37:1; Proverbs 24:1, 19). Ultimately, envy is a source of shame for those who have refused to walk in fellowship with God (Isaiah 26:11).

From a biblical perspective, *envy* can be described as "the feeling of displeasure produced by witnessing or hearing of the advantage or prosperity of others."[1] Wherever this term is used in Scripture, it is almost always in an evil sense. For example, the chief priests delivered Jesus to die out of a motive of envy (Matthew 27:18; Mark 15:10). While envy ranks right alongside murder and lying as characteristics of the pagan (Romans 1:29), it is also found among those who follow and serve Christ, usually as a response to someone else's prominence (Philippians 1:16), financial success (1 Timothy 6:4), the simple, old-nature characteristic of angry ill-will (Titus 3:3), or pride and a sense of entitlement (James 4:5).

According to the apostle Peter, the ultimate answer to envy, just as with deception, evil conversation, and hypocrisy, is to replace such vices with the pure spiritual food of the Bible, God's Word (1 Peter 2:1–2). According to Paul, envy originates in our old sinful human nature and must be replaced by the fruit of the Spirit (Galatians 5:21–23). Jealous emotions should have no place in the walk of the believer (Romans 13:13) for they evidence dependence on self rather than on God's Spirit and lead to confusion (1 Corinthians 3:3; James 3:16). James underscored the connection between jealousy and bitterness (James 3:14) and showed how closely such emotions are tied to self-deception.

Just as it was for Miriam, envy, or jealousy, is a frequent cause of prodigal behavior for many believers. Stan and Steve had attended seminary together. Close friends, they and their wives had frequently enjoyed outings together. They had prayed with each other over the difficulties of seminary life and had rejoiced with each other when both had been called to serve as pastors.

At first, Stan's ministry experienced a measure of growth in a suburban church which had been stagnant for years. This brought him a measure of acclaim among his former seminary classmates. After several years, however, his church hit a plateau, then began to decline. In the meantime, Steve had planted a new church in a predominantly rural area. For the first five years he pastored, the work was discouraging. Then suddenly the area became a suburban mecca for young families as a nearby metropolitan area flourished, and the church began to grow like a prairie fire. Over a five-year period, the church tripled in size, growing eventually to a congregation numbering well over a thousand by the end of a decade. As this growth occurred, Steve was in great demand as a speaker at seminars on church growth and became a guest on numerous radio and television talk shows. He even wrote a book on the growth of his church.

During this same time, however, Stan began to have less and less contact with his formerly close friend and even began criticizing the "worldly measures" he considered to be the primary reason for the growth of his colleague's church.

Could it be that Stan's charge of worldly measures, like Miriam's accusation of a mixed marriage, was actually a front to cover bitter feelings of jealousy?

Evidence of Envy

How can we tell if we are affected by envy? Three key words can help us detect its presence: *criticism, comparison,* and *contentment.*

The envious person is frequently critical of others, viewing their achievements and even their persons with a jaundiced eye. Such an individual finds it difficult to hand out a compliment, easy to pass out a criticism directly, and perhaps even easier to gossip indirectly.

The envious man or woman frequently finds himself or herself comparing roles and achievements with others. Did someone else get the raise I deserved? Was his raise larger? Has she been shown more favoritism by the boss? Did the company president take him to lunch twice in the last six months and only invite me along once? Were her ideas published while mine were overlooked? Did he get the choice plum of the business trip, spending two February weeks in southern Florida while I was assigned to North Dakota?

In a sense this comparative nature of envy may seem like fairness gone awry, an overemphasis on personal rights and entitlement or even a strong desire for control.

At the heart of envy is a failure to implement the principle of contentment. The apostle Paul said, "I have learned in whatever state I am, to be content" (Philippians 4:11). Dissatisfaction has become as common in America as rain in Seattle or sunshine in Phoenix, and it isn't limited to those who are not Christians. Frequently, jealously rears its ugly head over who was selected for the solo part in the church cantata, who was recognized as the more popular Sunday school teacher, or even who lost the most weight in the post-holiday diet derby.

Moses' Measured Response

Meek and humble man that he was, Moses must have felt the pain of Miriam's jealous betrayal, and his wife probably did as well. Undoubtedly both of them shed tears over the situation. Yet Moses chose not to defend himself against the jealous accusations. Instead he waited for God to act. Perhaps as he waited, he prayed.

That's the approach Floyd took, as he told a nationwide radio audience of the broken relationship caused by the envy of his own sister. He had been seriously ill when, in an angry huff, she told him she didn't care if he lived or died. "It really hurt me," he said, his breaking voice indicating the depths of the pain he felt. "I don't know what I can do."

In Floyd's life, it didn't take long for the conflict to be resolved. Within a month he phoned back to tell how God had dealt with her and had brought about repentance and reunion.

The Lord also moved swiftly to deal with Miriam. He summoned the three leaders to the tabernacle (the large tent which served as the center of worship), came down in a pillar of cloud, and instructed Miriam and Aaron to step closer.

Then He said, "Hear now My words: If there is a prophet among you, I, the Lord, make Myself known to him in a vision, and I speak to him in a dream. Not so with My servant Moses; he is faithful in all My house. I speak with him face-to-face, even plainly, and not in dark sayings; and he sees the form of the Lord" (Numbers 12:6–8; compare Deuteronomy 34:10). Because of his humility, his obedience, and the faithful way he carried out the responsibilities God had given him, Moses received God's revelation in a way no one else in the Old Testament did.

God's anger with Miriam and Aaron was clear from the pointed question with which He concluded the interview, "Why then were you not afraid to speak against My servant Moses?"

The Fear of the Lord

Clearly, the one ingredient missing from Miriam's life at this point was the fear of the Lord. Perhaps over the decades she had become confident in her leadership ability, complacent in her walk with the Lord, and even calloused regarding the rare privilege God had afforded her to lead His people.

Recently our colleague Warren Wiersbe delivered a chapel message at Back to the Bible that would have benefited Miriam. It certainly provided us with an important reminder. Speaking on the service of the priests and Levites in the Old Testament, Dr. Wiersbe raised the question, "If ministry were a matter of life or death, how would we respond?" Pointing to the numerous instances in which priests and Levites were reminded that their service was rendered "to Me," Dr. Wiersbe observed how frequently these servants of God were reminded to do their work with clean hands and pure hearts. Even in disassembling the tabernacle for travel, they were warned against even a casual glance at the holy instruments of worship, lest they die (Numbers 4:20).

Leprous Consequences

Suddenly the cloud lifted. The Lord's presence had departed. When Aaron turned to look at his sister, he was shocked to discover she was white as snow, suddenly infected with an advanced case of leprosy.

In horror, Aaron turned to his younger brother, "Oh, my lord! Please do not lay this sin on us, in which we have done foolishly and in which we have sinned. Please do not let her be as one dead, whose flesh is half consumed when he comes out of his mother's womb!" (Numbers 12:11–12). Aaron's cry was typical of the plea of many, including some prominent leaders who have yielded to the temptation and followed a prodigal path. Aaron voiced an honest confession of sin. At the same time, he asked that the consequence of her sin be lifted.

God always promises forgiveness. He never fails to delight in the honest confession of His children and in restoring them to fellowship. But He doesn't always choose to lift the natural consequences of sinful behavior. This is an important principle for those in spiritual leadership to recognize, especially in light of Paul's exhortation to publicly rebuke elders who sin so that others may also fear (1 Timothy 5:20).

Compassionate man that he was, Moses responded to Aaron's request by expressing a prayer for God's immediate healing. Yet God viewed her offense as serious. After all, she had initiated a rebellion against God's chosen servant. She would have to live with her consequences for a time, then she would be restored to fellowship.

Outside the Camp

So Miriam, leader of the women of Israel, found herself banished from the camp, forced to join other lepers and outcasts for seven lonely days and nights.

Since leprosy was perhaps the most dreaded disease of the day, infections of this kind were to be dealt with by careful inspection, enforced quarantine, and ceremonial declarations of cleansing when a person was found not to have leprosy.[2] The Mosaic Law clearly spelled out the terms of the quarantine in Leviticus 13:43–46.

As Miriam looked at her whitened, ravaged body, she must have been reminded of the seriousness of her sin and its dreadful consequences. As she used her voice to cry out the warning "Unclean! Unclean!" to anyone who approached her, she must have recalled using that voice on another day in another place to lead in joyous praise for God's great deliverance. During the lonely nights, she may have looked from the nearby hills at the pillar of fire hovering over the tabernacle. Once crowds had sought her; as a prophetess, she had spoken for God. Now she felt abandoned and disgraced because all the inhabitants of the tents she saw knew of her sin and its punishment.

When seven days had passed, God graciously healed Miriam. Her brother Aaron, the high priest, inspected her, and she was admitted to the camp again. She could have been punished with death or a lifetime of suffering and rejection. Graciously, God had limited the consequence of her sin. She rejoined the camp, and the Israelites began to move again.

Miriam had been especially gifted by God and more highly honored than any woman up to that time. God had designated her a prophetess, commissioned her to serve with her brothers in leading the people of Israel. She had served Him faithfully for many years, but as she came to think of herself more highly than she should have, she gradually slipped into the prodigal path of envy (see Romans 12:3). Then her honor turned to shame when she lost the right to use her gift and fulfill her leadership role. She provided living proof of the importance of the warning voiced by the apostle Paul, "Therefore let him who thinks he stands take heed lest he fall" (1 Corinthians 10:12). We are given no further details of the final days of Miriam's life. She probably continued to serve the Lord, perhaps in a very humble way. Some have suggested that she may have lost her zest for living and died of a broken heart just before the Israelites entered the Promised Land. What a serious warning she provides of the consequences of prodigal behavior. For most of her life, she ran the race well. Then Satan found an opening, an advantage, in that all-too-human tendency toward jealousy. And the results were devastating. Let's guard our hearts from bitterness and jealousy so we can end the race of life well.

Show Me My Secret Sins

Searcher of hearts, from mine erase
all thoughts that should not be,
And in its deep recesses trace,
My gratitude to Thee.

—George P. Morris

Endnotes

1. W. E. Vine, *An Expository Dictionary of New Testament Words* (Nashville: Thomas Nelson, 1984), 367.

2. For more information, see "Leper," *The International Standard Bible Encyclopedia* (Grand Rapids: Eerdmanns Publishing Co.), 3:1867–1868.

CHAPTER THIRTEEN

Samson: The High Price of Illicit Passion

Lust is the ape that gibbers in our loins. Tame him as we will by day, he rages all the wilder in our dreams by night. Just when we think we're safe from him, he raises up his ugly head and smirks, and there's no river in the world flows cold and strong enough to strike him down.

—Frederick Buechner, *Godric*

The question is not whether we have sexual desire, but whether sexual desire has us.

—E. Stanley Jones, *Victorious Living*

He was a man with a unique opportunity, born at a time when Israel was politically oppressed by surrounding nations while spiritually and morally deteriorating from within. He had godly parents and a special gift of power from the Holy Spirit during most of his life. Tragically, however, Samson never gained control of the one power that overshadowed even his incredible physical strength. He never learned to control himself. His physical strength was overmatched by his moral weakness, and Samson became a prodigal whose life ended in tragedy.

We tend to picture Samson as the typical Hollywood strongman—robust, muscular, with long, wavy hair. He may have looked like some of the male models who appear on the covers of romantic novels, in television commercials for female perfumes, or like those muscular masters of hand-to-hand combat who are featured in action-adventure movies. Samson must have been the heartthrob of many Israelite women and apparently of more than a few Philistine women as well.

His Achilles' heel was lust. Samson had a weakness for women, a weakness that eventually did him in.

Godly Parents

Samson's life started out well but took a downhill turn, a prodigal path from which he never recovered until the very end of his life. However, his downfall could not be blamed on his parents. They had eagerly anticipated his arrival. They genuinely loved him, and they must have modeled for him the same fear of God they displayed when they learned from an angel that they were about to become parents of the world's strongest man.

One day, the Lord sent an angel to Samson's mother, promising that she would conceive a son. The messenger warned that the child would be dedicated to God from the womb and designated to deliver Israel from oppressive tribute and subjugation at the hands of the Philistines.

When she told her husband, Manoah, about the messenger, he was puzzled and skeptical. But when he prayed to God, the angel returned, giving both parents detailed instructions about how to raise their son.

When he was born, they followed the angel's directive, raising Samson according to the Nazarite vows. A Nazarite—the term simply means "one consecrated to God"—was to abstain from drinking any fermented beverage, from cutting his hair, or from coming in contact with dead bodies (Numbers 6:2–6). Although such vows were typically taken for a limited period of time, Samson's was to be a lifetime vow (Judges 13:7). He was a man whose mission in life was to deliver his people. As he grew up against a backdrop of forty years without any evidence of God's power in Israel, Samson must have heard from his godly parents about God's purpose in his life, how he had been the one chosen to deliver Israel from the dominating hand of the Philistines.

Unfortunately, neither exceptional ability nor a divine calling gives assurance of fulfilled potential for serving God—nor does the presence of godly parents. This is one of the most important lessons we can learn from the life of Samson. Here was a man with incredible potential, unique gifts, and rare abilities. Yet despite his personal abilities and the input of his godly parents, Samson in great measure failed to fulfill his awesome potential.

Early in his life, people recognized that Phil had an amazing ability to communicate with people, plus a personal magnetism that drew others to him. His Christian parents, his pastor, and others all applauded when he decided to train for the ministry. After attending college and seminary, he pastored a succession of churches, ultimately winding up as the senior pastor of a large, fast-growing church in an affluent suburb of a major Southern city.

However, one day a staff member caught him coming out of the elevator of a local hotel with a female member of his church, a woman he had been counseling. An investigation revealed that Phil had been sexually involved with this woman and with several others as well. Despite his awesome talent and years of training, a lack of personal integrity had led to a moral downfall and personal disgrace. Like Samson, Phil failed to fulfill his potential for service to God.

Sleeping with the Enemy

The Philistines were a powerful Aryan people that settled along the coastal strip of southwest Palestine. They presented an ongoing threat to the Israelite nation and actually dominated Israel because of their ability to smelt and forge iron weapons and to keep those weapons out of the hands of their enemies.[1] By the time Samson appeared on the scene, the land of Israel had been overrun by these warlike enemies for about forty years.

Rather than considering the Philistines as the enemies of his people and Israel's God, however, it seems that Samson viewed them as a people with whom he could fraternize and as a source of sensual pleasure. As a young man he visited the city of Timnah where he spotted a young Philistine woman. When he returned home, he insisted that his father and mother arrange for him to marry her since such arrangements were the custom of the day.

Surprisingly, the parents who before had been models of godliness, raised only a mild objection to a union that would clearly violate

God's law—"Aren't there any young Israelite women that strike your fancy? Must you get a wife from the uncircumcised Philistines?" But Samson insisted, and his parents relented. Even though Samson was already moving in a prodigal direction, God would use his lust-motivated behavior to bring ruin upon the Philistines.

On the way to arrange the wedding, Samson wandered off into a nearby vineyard where he encountered a young lion. As God's Spirit moved upon him with power, he tore the lion apart with his bare hands. When he later returned for the wedding celebration, he found the lion's carcass occupied by a swarm of honeybees.

During the marriage feast, he presented a riddle and offered a bet to the thirty Philistine men chosen by his bride as wedding attendants: a suit of clothing to each one if they could solve a riddle during the seven days of the feast. If no one could solve it, Samson would receive thirty suits of clothing. "Okay," they said. "Let's hear the riddle."

"Out of the eater came something to eat,
and out of the strong came something sweet."

Unable to solve the riddle and faced with the possible humiliation of losing the wager, the Philistines pressured Samson's bride to wheedle the answer out of him. After she had wept petulantly every day of the wedding feast, Samson finally gave in to her manipulation and explained to her about the lion he had killed. She passed the answer on to the wedding guests who gave him the answer on the final day of the feast. Realizing what had happened, he responded, "If you had not plowed with my heifer, you would not have solved my riddle!" (Judges 14:18).

Furious at their deception, Samson angrily left the celebration without taking his bride along. To pay his debt, he attacked the Philistine city of Ashkelon about twenty-five miles to the southeast. Empowered by the Spirit, he killed thirty Philistine men and took their clothing to cover his wager.

Though his actions were clearly those of a man who was about as far out of fellowship with God as he could be, the Lord used what he did to drive a wedge between Israel and Philistia that would ultimately lead to the overthrow of the Philistines.

Blazing Foxes

At first, Samson refused to return to Timnah for his wife. Later, when he showed up to claim her, he discovered her father had annulled the marriage and given her to another man. Livid with anger, Samson returned home to tell his Israelite friends, "This time I shall be blameless regarding the Philistines if I harm them" (Judges 15:3).

When his Israelite companions refused to help him, Samson enlisted the unwitting help of some animals. Capturing three hundred "foxes"—probably a type of jackal common to that portion of Palestine—Samson took the foxes two at a time and tied their tails together with a torch in the middle. Then, setting the torches on fire, he released them into the Philistine's wheat fields.

This incident took place during May just when the fields were ripe with wheat. It had probably been about two months since any significant rain had fallen, and the grain was quite dry. Crazed with fear and pain, the foxes fled throughout the dry fields, igniting fire after fire which consumed not only the wheat fields but also the extensive vineyards and olive groves. As a result, the three main crops of the Philistines were completely destroyed.

When the Philistines retaliated by burning Samson's intended wife and her father to death, Samson retreated to a rock cave and plotted further revenge. Sadly, an innocent Israelite village, Lehi, found itself surrounded by angry Philistine soldiers. It was a classic reminder that the cycle of revenge is a vicious one indeed and frequently draws innocent people into its web who may simply be nearby and have nothing to do with the original hatred or animosity between the warring factions.

Lethal Jawbone

The men of Lehi who came to meet with Samson had become so conditioned to the yoke of Philistine bondage that they preferred to turn Samson over to the Philistines rather than allow him to lead them into battle to overthrow these enemies of God and the people of Israel.

The Israelites bound Samson with two new ropes and led him out to the Philistines. As they moved toward the Philistines, the Spirit of the Lord infused Samson with strength, and he broke the ropes like they were spaghetti. Grabbing the first weapon available—the jawbone of a dead donkey—Samson used it to kill a thousand Philistines. It was to be the high point of his life in more ways than one.

Suddenly realizing how thirsty he was, Samson called out to the Lord in prayer, "You have given this great deliverance by the hand of Your servant; and now shall I die of thirst and fall into the hand of the uncircumcised?" His prayer prompted God to respond by opening a hollow place in a rock which immediately filled with water. The place came to be called *En Hakkore* or "the spring of the caller."

We identify this as the high point of Samson's twenty-year career as a leader in Israel because here he clearly acknowledged his dependence upon God to sustain and empower him.

Downhill Road

Sadly, although there were still victories ahead, the road from this point on wound downhill.

Samson, now acknowledged as Israel's leader, became the object of Philistine dread. Unafraid of his enemies, he demonstrated both his brashness and his unbridled passion by visiting a prostitute who kept an inn in Gaza, the well-fortified capital of Philistia. After his assignation with the prostitute, Samson got up at midnight, went to the barred gates of the city, ripped out the doors of the gate, lifted them on his shoulders, and started walking home.

This action caused great humiliation for the Philistines. After all, the gates of a city were the symbol of its strength. If someone could actually take possession of the gates of his enemy, he had won a major victory. By carrying the gates of Gaza to the top of the hill that looked toward Hebron, the major city in Judah, Samson even more deeply humbled his enemies.

Despite winning such an amazing victory over the enemies of God, Samson continued to fail in his battle with personal lust. A short time later, he became involved with a Philistine woman named Delilah, who may have been a temple prostitute in the worship of the god Dagon. Samson thought he was in love with Delilah, but his relationship with her would lead to his personal downfall and the end of his service to the Lord.

Understanding his weakness for women, the chiefs of the cities of Philistia offered Delilah an exorbitant bribe if she would entice Samson, learn the source of his great strength, and find out how he could be overpowered. So the woman he thought he loved readily agreed to sell him out for money.

But fun-loving Samson considered this just another game like the earlier riddle. He was so self-confident that even though he understood how the Philistines were trying to use Delilah, he teased her with several false answers—bow strings, unused ropes, even weaving the locks of his head—as he skirted ever closer to the edge of disaster.

Meanwhile, Delilah persisted in her efforts to manipulate him. "How can you say, 'I love you,' when your heart is not with me? You have mocked me these three times, and have not told me where your great strength lies" (Judges 16:15). As she pleaded, begged, argued, and cajoled him day after day, Samson's resistance was finally worn down. Without considering the consequences, he told her the truth.

The Secret of His Strength

Explaining his Nazarite vow, he gave her a "secularized" version of the source of his strength. "It's my hair," he pointed out. Unfortunately, Samson was only telling her half the story. The real secret of his great strength came from the power of God, to which he had access as long as he kept his Nazarite vow. Cutting his hair was just an outward symbol of the inward disobedience to the vow in his heart.

In short order, the leaders of the Philistines arrived, money in hand, and Delilah cut off Samson's hair. When he awoke, he thought he would simply shake himself free, just like before. Tragically, he didn't realize that the Lord's power had departed from him.

So it is with us. It is obedience to God, not religious appearances, that gives us access to the power of God. It is essential that we combine both inward and outward purity. For a long time, Samson had been morally unclean. That uncleanness had taken its toll, even though he seemed outwardly to enjoy as many victories as before.

Raised in a Christian home, Jules had always been seen as a paragon of virtue, a tower of spiritual and physical strength. Early in life he committed himself to the Lord, letting everyone know of his plans to follow his father's footsteps into ministry. He began preaching at an early age and was recognized as uniquely gifted. Some called him a "powerhouse for God." He was also successful in competing in several sports at his Christian high school and college.

Yet Jules nurtured a secret weakness which he had cultivated since his early teenage years when he had worked as a janitor at a neighborhood store. As he cleaned the building one evening, Jules discovered a hiding place where the men who ran the store kept a supply of pornographic magazines. He began gradually, but with increasing frequency, to spend a portion of his work time scrutinizing the pictures that his conscience told him he had no business seeing.

During high school, Jules developed the habit of slipping into X-rated movies which he was able to do because he looked mature for his age. Soon his sexual obsession demanded even more, and he began slipping out in the evening, looking into the windows of nearby homes.

After several close calls during his college years—incidents in which he was almost caught but was able to redirect suspicion—Jules was finally confronted as he furtively watched one of the girls on campus through the window of her dorm. It became a lasting blight on the rising career of one who had been recognized by all who knew him to have incredible potential. And it all happened, ultimately, because years before he had chosen to follow the prodigal path of lust.

Tragic Consequences

For Samson, the consequences he experienced were both immediate and permanent. The Philistines sadistically blinded him, bound him with bronze leg irons, and forced him to turn a mill wheel in the city of Gaza.

During his previous trip to Gaza, Samson had used his eyes to enjoy the pleasures of sin with a prostitute (Judges 16:1). Then he had employed his God-given strength to remove the city gates. This time he was brought back to the city without sight or great strength and was forced to fulfill what was normally the job of an animal or a slave, turning the millstone to grind grain in the Philistine prison.

Samson's final degradation was much like the consequences experienced by those who choose to live as prodigals today. Untold numbers of men and women experience physical pain, an inability to have children, or a host of other physical as well as emotional consequences of the more than fifty sexually transmitted diseases that affect people today.

It's important to understand that sin is sin. God doesn't hold one sin up as morally or spiritually worse than any other. However, Scripture makes it clear that there are unique and drastic consequences to sexual immorality. That's why Paul instructed Christians to flee from immoral behavior (1 Corinthians 6:18). As the apostle explained, the individual who commits immorality is actually sinning against his own body.

During the course of our ministry, we have talked with literally hundreds of men and women from all walks of life who've experienced these tragic consequences. Some have contracted AIDS or another sexually transmitted disease. Others have found themselves facing the dilemma brought on by pregnancy outside of marriage. Many have found their marriages shattered and their relationships with spouses and children devastated by the betrayal of trust. Almost all have suffered the intense emotional pain of guilt, rejection, and betrayal brought on by violating the clear moral principles spelled out in God's Word.

There's another lesson to be learned from the consequences which befell Samson at this critical point in his life. Those who feel entitled and who seek to fulfill those feelings by manipulating others are often the most susceptible to manipulation themselves. So it was with Israel's strongman. He had made a career of manipulating the people around him in order to get what he wanted. Now his archenemies, the Philistines, had used Delilah—whom he had also used for personal gratification—to get back at him and to ultimately deprive him of his God-given strength.

Jesus once told His disciples that those who live by the sword would die by the sword. Perhaps we could paraphrase that by saying that those who advance by manipulation will often find themselves falling as a result of manipulation.

Finally, the Philistines felt they were secure. Samson would never again pose a threat to them. There was no way he could fulfill the mission he had been born to achieve. Once he had felt so strong that he considered himself beyond capture. Now he had been blinded and bound in chains.

Up to this point, Samson had been spiritually blinded by his sensuality. Now physically blinded by his enemy, he undoubtedly began to remember the God he had forsaken, the God of the vow of his youth. The weakness he experienced when his hair was cut began to dissipate. As his hair grew back and as he meditated on God during his endless hours of grinding, his strength returned. Unfortunately for them, his captors failed to realize what was happening.

Final Victory

One day the Philistines held a great feast to honor the god they claimed had given them victory over their enemy, Samson. In the height of their drunken celebration, they brought their prize captive, still chained, from his prison. Samson was taken into the Philistine temple, a long inner chamber ringed with many side chambers. At the center stood two massive pillars which supported the roof at the center of the building. About three thousand people were standing on the flat roof surface, watching the spectacle. There could have been another nine or ten thousand inside the building itself. Led about by a little boy, Samson asked, "Let me feel the pillars which support the temple, so I can lean on them" (Judges 16:26).

Finally, Samson again called on the Lord. It was only the second recorded prayer of a man who had started out with such great potential.

As the crowd jeered at the captive and praised their pagan god, Samson cried out to the God of Israel, "O Lord God, remember me, I pray! Strengthen me, I pray, just this once, O God, that I may with one blow take vengeance on the Philistines for my two eyes!" (Judges 16:28).

Perhaps no one noticed as Samson grasped the two middle pillars that supported the temple, bracing himself against them. Perhaps there was a lull in the revelry when Samson cried out with a loud voice, "Let me die with the Philistines!" Pushing with all his might, he shoved the pillars off their pedestals. The flat roof, filled with Philistines, fell down onto the crowd inside, killing everyone, including Samson.

The temple was demolished. The leaders of the Philistines were dead, and the political power of the Philistine people was diminished. In his death, Samson had killed more Philistines than he had in an entire lifetime.

It was a remarkable ending for the life of a man who chose the prodigal path of personal lust. From the beginning, he had been given a commission to liberate his people from the yoke of Philistine bondage. God had ultimately granted Samson the power of His Spirit and the strength to carry out that commission.

Yet Samson had treated his gifts lightly. Refusing to acknowledge his own weaknesses, he consorted with many women, indulged himself in the passions of the flesh, and even dallied with the enemies of God. Most serious of all, Samson forgot that his strength was not his own, but God's. In the end, he lost his calling, his joy, his strength, his use of God's power, and eventually his life.

Each of us has been given gifts, unique abilities for God-given service. God expects us to treat them with reverence, to use them with humble commitment, and to understand and fulfill His purpose for our lives.

To misuse God's abilities, to ignore them, to allow our lives to be dominated by the Enemy doesn't remove us from being God's children. Nor does it mean God will never use us again. But it does place us in grave danger of sliding down the slope of prodigal behavior and of suffering the sad consequences of spiritual and personal potential unused.

Endnotes

1. Merrill F. Unger, *Unger's Bible Dictionary*, 3d edition (Chicago: Moody Press, 1966), 859–860.

PART THREE

Modern Prodigals and Those Who Love Them

Turn Your Heart Toward Home

Late in the evening when ev'ryone was sleeping,
the father of the wayward son slipped out in the night;
He looked toward the city and wiped away his tears,
and prayed his son could hear his father's cry:
Turn your heart toward home, turn your heart toward home,
you've been gone so long, turn your heart toward home.

Not only the sons are the wayward ones,
there are mothers and fathers who have said their good-byes;
In the sad eyes of children looking through their tears,
praying mom and daddy could hear their cry:
Turn your heart toward home, turn your heart toward home,
you've been gone so long, turn your heart toward home.

There are those who have never walked away from home,
but in their hearts they're so many miles away;
And the Father in heaven is the only one who knows,
if they listen they could hear Him say:
Turn your heart toward home, turn your heart toward home,
you've been gone so long, turn your heart toward home.
You've been gone so long, please don't wait too long,
turn your heart toward home.

171

CHAPTER FOURTEEN

Will God Take Me Back?

God doesn't hold the past against you, He holds the future ahead of you.

—Author Unknown

Sharon was weeping uncontrollably. A bright, vivacious teenager who had grown up in a Christian home, she had been the kind of young person no one would have expected to have trouble. But Sharon got caught up in a relationship with a man ten years older than she was, and now she was pregnant.

Her strict parents had reacted to her condition with horror and outrage. Feeling betrayed and bitter when they learned of a relationship that had been kept secret from them, they angrily rejected Sharon's request for forgiveness.

As she sat on the couch in the parsonage, tears pouring from her eyes, Sharon told her pastor and his wife, "My parents have told me they cannot forgive me. I don't blame them. If they can't take me back, how could I possibly expect God to do so? After all, He's perfect."

Sharon's question plagues many modern-day prodigals. It is a major reason why a large number of them never turn from their prodigal way to come back to the Lord. Time after time, both of us have heard individuals voice some variation of the theme, "I just don't think God can ever forgive me. What I have done has taken me beyond the possibility that He would ever take me back."

Quite frankly, nothing could be further from the truth. There is absolutely nothing you or I can do, no sin we can commit, that places us beyond God's forgiveness and restoration to fellowship with Him. This is not to say there will not be consequences to sinful behavior or that those consequences will not make both restoration and life difficult. But the Bible makes it absolutely clear: God forgives any and all who turn to Him.

An Ironclad Promise

We can count on the fact that God always lovingly welcomes every prodigal who sincerely turns to Him in repentance and desires forgiveness and restoration. It's an ironclad promise, given by Jesus when He said, "The one who comes to Me I will by no means cast out" (John 6:37).

There's a basis for this startling assertion. It's found in an important observation we made as we examined the parable of the prodigal son. There was never a time when the young man even considered the possibility that his father would refuse his return: not when he left, not when he was enjoying his prodigal lifestyle, and certainly not when the consequences of his rebellious ways overwhelmed him. Not even in the pigpen did the thought ever enter his mind that his father would refuse to welcome him back.

The sins you and I commit may be great. The prodigal path we follow may take us a long way down into shame and even despair. But God's grace is still sufficient to lift us from the pit of failure and restore us to fellowship with Him. And just as the Bible has many examples of prodigals, it is equally rich in examples of God's forgiveness and His power to restore.

David learned this truth the hard way. The "sweet singer of Israel" and "the man after God's own heart" committed adultery and murder. Yet he wrote:

I waited patiently for the Lord; and He inclined to me, and heard my cry. He also brought me up out of a horrible pit, out of the miry clay, and set my feet upon a rock, and established my steps. He has put a new song in my mouth—praise to our God; many will see it and fear, and will trust in the Lord.
—Psalm 40:1–3

David's words vividly describe the "pit of horrors" into which this godly man fell and the gracious manner in which God rescued him. How refreshing to be reminded that despite a massive failure, God's ability to restore and forgive is always equal to the task.

Nor is David the only example of such grace in the Bible. Judah, one of Jacob's sons, sold his younger brother into slavery and lied to his father, suggesting that Joseph had been killed by a wild animal. The forgiveness Judah and his brothers later received from Joseph clearly mirrored the forgiveness God extends to us as well. Judah became father of the tribe from which Jesus, "the Lion of the tribe of Judah" and the author of our forgiveness, would ultimately come.

In the New Testament era John Mark was a quitter. He refused to stay with Paul and Barnabas during a difficult portion of their first missionary journey. As a result, Paul was ready to write him off. Yet through the encouragement of Barnabas and the work of God in his life, John Mark was restored to fellowship. He ultimately received the stamp of approval from the apostle Paul himself as "useful to me for ministry" (2 Timothy 4:11). More importantly, he received God's stamp of forgiveness, restoration, and approval when he became the human author of the book we now know as the gospel of Mark.

"But how can I know God will take me back?" you say. "My mind wants to believe, but I just feel there's no way." We'd like to suggest a fourfold foundation for your hope that God will take you back.

The Character of God

First, base your hope of restoration on the character of God.

The Scriptures paint a picture of a God who is holy and sovereign but who is also characterized by loyal love, mercy, and longsuffering. Since our concept of God is often colored by our own experiences, especially that of early life, many of us tend to see God in one of two extremes. For some, who were given any and everything, God is simply viewed like the genie from Disney's popular movie, *Aladdin*—a cosmic servant whose primary function and purpose is to give us whatever we desire or feel entitled to whenever we want it.

The other extreme to which people swing is to view God as an eternal killjoy, some kind of tyrannical, grandfather-like being sitting on a throne in heaven, reaching down to club people into submission and delighting in exacting just as much punishment as He can whenever we go astray.

Neither of these concepts is accurate at all. Perhaps the biblical person who provides us with the most balanced view of God's character was an individual who initially experienced many ups and downs; however, Peter finally found stability and a living hope in his relationship with the loving Father. Peter began his first letter to fellow believers with a note of praise to God the Father who "according to His abundant mercy has begotten us again to a living hope through the resurrection of Jesus Christ from the dead" (1 Peter 1:3). It is that abundant mercy to which Peter directs his reader as he concludes his second letter with a warning of coming judgment. Responding to critics who have suggested there will be no judgment since it hasn't happened yet, Peter responds by explaining why judgment has been delayed.

> The Lord is not slack concerning His promise, as some count slackness, but is longsuffering toward us, not willing that any should perish but that all should come to repentance.
> —2 Peter 3:9

From his exposure to the Son who mirrored the Father and from his own personal experience as a prodigal, Peter learned just how longsuffering the Father could be. While his statement is especially directed toward unbelievers, it has strong implications for believers who are living prodigal lives as well.

The Old Testament presents an equally positive picture of the longsuffering, tender mercy, and loyal love of God in an obscure book named Lamentations. It records the grief experienced by the prophet

Jeremiah as he watched his beloved city, Jerusalem, fall to the conquering Babylonians. As he took pen in hand to write this prophetic dirge, Jeremiah cried out to God, describing in graphic detail why he felt like giving up and how he felt that God had removed all hope.

Then suddenly, almost as if someone had switched on a massive spotlight in the absolute darkness of a subterranean cave, Jeremiah wrote:

> This I recall to my mind, therefore I have hope. Through the Lord's mercies we are not consumed, because His compassions fail not. They are new every morning; great is Your faithfulness.
> —Lamentations 3:21–23

While nothing in his circumstances could have renewed Jeremiah's hope, three great truths about the character of God revealed in these verses totally changed his perspective.

First, Jeremiah recognized God's loyal love. This beautiful concept, wrapped up in the Hebrew word *hesed* found throughout the Old Testament, shows how God has chosen to be loyal and loving without any regard to the present character or past failures of Israel. God could justly do this because of the redemption He would ultimately provide, a redemption pictured in the Old Testament sacrifices.

Next, Jeremiah thought about the Lord's tender compassions. Unlike humans, who often have no feeling for others who suffer, God is touched with the feeling of our pain. All too frequently, prodigal behavior is related to pain and hurt that no one else even knows about or understands. It isn't excused by the pain, but it is explained by the hurt. Without question, our compassionate heavenly Father understands better and cares more than anyone else.

The third important truth Jeremiah recalled was the Lord's incredible faithfulness which he described as "great." We might even translate this verse "*massive* is Your faithfulness." Jeremiah's point was clear: no one could be trusted like the Lord to care for us, to feel with us, and to remain true to us, even when we have failed to remain true to Him. That's how He responded to the prodigal nation Israel, and He responds the same way to us. That's why Jeremiah could move from bitter disappointment to an encouraging trust. The Lord would always be there for His children, no matter what the circumstances.

God the Father will never go against His own compassionate character, nor will He forget His promises. He will welcome you with open arms, just as the father in Jesus' parable so enthusiastically welcomed his prodigal son.

The Compassion of Christ

When you wonder whether God will take you back, a second important factor to consider is the compassion of God's Son, Jesus Christ. Not only did the Father so love the world that He gave His Son, Jesus cared enough to lay down His life for us (John 15:13). Jesus never violated any aspect of the Law even though none of us could keep it (John 8:46). He was totally without guilt, yet He willingly took the punishment we deserved, endured the physical torment, the emotional pain, and above all, the spiritual anguish of separation from His Father, all because of His love for us.

Even as He affirmed the extent of His love for His friends as they reclined around the table at the Last Supper (John 15:13), Jesus knew that to some degree each of these men would become a prodigal before the next day dawned. Judas would betray Him, the others would flee in terror for their lives. And Peter, the group's acknowledged leader, would deny Him with an oath.

If Christ could sustain an unconditional love for His disciples under these circumstances, there is no question of His ongoing love for us. No matter what your failure, no matter how you became a prodigal, He suffered for you, and He will never turn you away if you turn back to Him.

The Call of the Holy Spirit

A third factor to consider when you wonder whether God will take you back is the encouragement found in the call of the Holy Spirit.

During that meal we call the Last Supper, Jesus told His disciples that the Holy Spirit would be sent to provide them with the encouragement they needed for the trying times ahead (John 16:7).

Given the Spirit's ability to convince people of the reality and consequences of their alienation from God and to draw individuals to faith in Christ, could anyone be more uniquely qualified to pursue prodigals and draw them back to fellowship with the Lord? Since He is the one who guides us into all truth, isn't it logical to assume that He would be uniquely able to break through the deceit and denial that accompanies prodigal behavior? Since He is one with the Father and the Son, doesn't it stand to reason that He could best extend desperately-needed hope to those who feel there is no way out of their prodigal trap? And since He is the one uniquely designated to glorify Jesus, it seems appropriate that He is the one who can empower the prodigal to turn from the error of his or her way back to a walk that glorifies the Savior.

Certainly this seems to be the thrust of Paul's words of encouragement to early believers in the city of Rome. First, the apostle acknowledged his own tendency to struggle with prodigal behavior because of his old nature. "I know the right thing to do," he says in chapter 7 of his letter. "But so frequently I fail to do it. The sin nature in me causes me to fail to do what the true me wants to do."

"It's an internal warfare," he explains, "and it often makes me miserable."

The solution, as Paul goes on to explain, is to "not walk according to the flesh but according to the Spirit" (Romans 8:4). He is the one who transforms our thinking and behavior to make it possible for us to turn from the prodigal path and practice the righteousness of God.

After more than thirty references to "I" in the closing verses of chapter 7, Paul refers to the Spirit eight times in Romans 8. The old "I" is the key to prodigal behavior, and the Spirit is the key to that which glorifies God.

And since the Spirit's primary purpose is to glorify God by drawing people to Jesus and enabling them to reflect His glory, He would certainly never turn away a prodigal.

Confidence in God's Word

There's still a fourth line of evidence to affirm that God will always take a prodigal back: the clear statements of the Bible, God's Word. The Bible is filled with both promises and examples that affirm the validity of this truth.

- The Old Testament prophet Isaiah said, " 'Come now, and let us reason together,' says the Lord. 'Though your sins are like scarlet, they shall be as white as snow. Though they are red like crimson, they shall be as wool' " (Isaiah 1:18).
- Jesus invited, "Come to Me, all you who labor and are heavy laden, and I will give you rest. Take My yoke upon you and learn from Me, for I am gentle and lowly in heart, and you will find rest for your souls. For My yoke is easy and My burden is light" (Matthew 11:28–30).
- John the apostle provided a most encouraging promise: "If we confess our sins, He is faithful and just to forgive us our sins and to cleanse us from all unrighteousness" (1 John 1:9).

These and many other promises in the Bible affirm God's welcoming attitude toward prodigals. It's also affirmed by the many examples of

His loving concern and tender care for those who are weak, wandering, and lost that are found throughout the Bible.

Beginning with Adam and Eve, who were sought out by the Lord God after they hid in shame in the Garden, through the Old Testament failures of Abraham, Moses, David, Jonah, and others, and through the New Testament struggles of Peter and the other disciples, the pattern is the same—God's fatherly love follows the prodigal.

The parable of the prodigal son reinforces the Bible's overall message of the waywardness of prodigals and the gracious welcome that awaits them in the presence of a loving Father. Even though that Jewish father had another son at home, still his heart went out to the one who had wandered away. That lost son was of critical concern to his dad. Just as the lost coin was a priority to the woman who had ten coins and the missing sheep in the wilderness was of great concern to the shepherd who watched over the other ninety-nine, so this son occupied the heart of his father from the day he was gone until the day he returned.

You Matter to God

Friend, if you are involved in prodigal behavior, whether secret sins of the heart or the open sins of life, the heavenly Father still cares about you. He knows all about you, including your name, the details of your physical and emotional makeup, your activities of both today and yesterday, and even the thoughts and motives of your heart! He knows "where you're coming from." He accepts you for who you are and eagerly looks for you to turn to Him, waiting just as that human father waited for his wandering son.

He will never turn you away!

> I have decided to follow Jesus
> I have decided to follow Jesus
> I have decided to follow Jesus
> No turning back, no turning back.

—Unknown

CHAPTER FIFTEEN

Finding the Way Home

Home is a place where, when you have to go there, they have to take you in.
　　　　　　　　　—Robert Frost, *The Death of the Hired Man*

Ron had been a prodigal, no doubt about it. He fought a lot in school, getting into trouble on a regular basis. Under the influence of an older brother, he began sampling beer and developed a taste for it. Often Ron's weekends were a drunken blur. He dropped out of school, held several jobs, some with a relative degree of success, married twice, divorced twice, fathered two children, and generally as he put it, "Made a mess of most everything in my life."

Then in his mid-thirties, Ron the prodigal, who mostly lived in the streets and carried the pain, guilt, and shame of a ruined life, came to himself.

As he would later describe it, "I remembered a time as a teenager when I was visiting with my aunt and uncle, and my cousin and I went to a baseball game together. There, sitting about midway up in the stands on the first base side, somewhere around the sixth inning, I bowed my head and asked Jesus Christ to be my Savior and Lord.

"All those years, I'd wandered away from God, done things my own way, taken the popular approach to life. None of it had ever worked. What I needed was to come home. By home I don't mean a house in the country or the city or a place where my family lived. I mean home to my heavenly Father."

As Ron remembered it, his earthly home hadn't been a pleasant place. His parents had divorced while he was young, and he and his brothers and sister had suffered a great deal of hardship and grief. But as he looked back on it, he couldn't help reflecting, "The Lord never left me. I was never out of His sight, even though I tried to run away from Him.

"And I was miserable, miserable the whole way. Oh, I tried to kid myself, kill the pain with drinking and other kinds of things, but none of it ever worked. And nothing can compare with coming home!"

Your Way Back

Maybe you too once enjoyed that privileged position with God. Perhaps as a young child, maybe as a teenager or a young adult, you tasted of the waters of life. Placing your trust in the Savior who died for you and rose again, you began to enjoy the benefits of being part of God's family. Perhaps you experienced the joy of a Christian home and the encouragement of a church family where God's Word was taught and where Christians encouraged each other and strengthened each other in the faith.

Then a time came when you turned off the straight road of Christian faith. You decided to chart your course along the more popular road.

Maybe it was peer pressure, perhaps outright rebellion, or just the nagging restlessness that grows out of the old nature we all have. The point is, you went the wrong direction, and now you know it. Maybe it's just a nagging conviction, a sense of unease, or a general awareness that things aren't right. More likely, it's an outright certainty, especially if you've read through the book to this point. Now you're sure it's time for you to turn from the wrong way to the right way.

So what do you do?

The four steps we often recommend to prodigals aren't a bad place to start: honest confession, genuine repentance, absolute trust, and uncompromising obedience. These steps have worked for a multitude of prodigals from all walks of life. They can work for you.

Honest Confession

Before we can ever start down the right road, we have to admit that we're on the wrong road. Both of us have had times when we took a wrong turn driving to a speaking engagement, and both of us have been blessed with wives who cared enough to occasionally *suggest* that we *might* be headed in the wrong direction and that we *might benefit* from stopping to ask directions.

Neither of us is extremely fond of consulting our wives for geographic directions. Linda Kroll and Kathy Hawkins both have many talents, but we are convinced that we are generally better at reading a road map or finding directions than the women we married.

There have been times, however, when both of us have had to admit we were driving on the wrong road. What a difference it made when we finally were willing to acknowledge that we were lost!

That's what happens when we exercise honest confession. We're admitting we've taken a wrong turn, done some wrong things, things that displeased and hurt God and perhaps hurt others in the process.

For the person who has never trusted Christ as Savior, it means admitting that we are spiritually lost, that we are sinners incapable of saving ourselves. Even the good things we try to do in order to please God fall incredibly short of His perfect standard (Isaiah 64:6).

For the believer, it means exercising the responsibility—and privilege—the apostle John spoke of when he promised, "If we confess our sins, He is faithful and just to forgive us our sins and to cleanse us from all unrighteousness" (1 John 1:9). The apostle John's deep experience as one of Jesus' disciples had convinced him that God was absolutely perfect—He is totally "light" with no spiritual darkness. If we claim to live in fellowship with Him and at the same time walk in darkness, we are lying. But to the degree we walk in the light, as He is in the light, we experience fellowship and cleansing (vv. 6–7).

Tragically, there may be times when we deny our sinful actions. Sometimes we even deny the reality and influence of our sin nature. To do so, John says, is to engage in self-deception. Rather than being controlled by God's truth, we are like puppets pulled by the strings of our own self-deceit (v. 8).

The antidote is honest confession. That's the responsibility He places squarely on us. When we confess our waywardness, identify our failure, own our sin, and recognize its offensiveness toward God, then He faithfully and rightly forgives the sins we confess and cleanses us of all unrighteousness (v. 9).

Stop and think about why you feel so miserable. Reflect on your sense of remorse or your feelings of guilt. Remember, Satan wants to desensitize us to sin. He'd like to convince us it's not that serious. It only affects other people, and after awhile they'll get over it.

Yet as the prophet Isaiah observed in the Old Testament, sin is like the stench of an open sewer to God—it's an affront to His holy character. Not only is He rightly offended, but He also is grieved by our sin. We need to spend some serious time thinking about what that means.

We're not talking about the ongoing browbeating of false guilt that refuses to accept and acknowledge God's forgiveness. When we honestly confess our sins, He forgives us, cleans us up, and even gives us grace to walk in obedience. So even if we continue to struggle with the condemnation of false guilt, the God who knows us has declared us forgiven (1 John 3:20). How important it is for us to remember that honest confession brings forgiveness and restoration to fellowship!

Genuine Repentance

Honest confession also leads to the change of mind that produces a change of life. When we have confessed sin and experienced forgiveness, we have confidence in our relationship with God that not only will He answer our prayers in His own perfect way but He will also empower us to obey Him as well (1 John 3:21–22). It's important that we consciously replace faulty thinking patterns about false guilt or conditional love with those based on the truth of God's complete forgiveness and unconditional love.

For the person who hasn't trusted Christ as Savior, this means turning from whatever religious system, personal works, or false way we have been following and placing our trust in Christ alone as the only way to be right with God. For the believer, it means acknowledging that we have been headed down the wrong road and that now it's time for that change of mind that leads to an authentic change of life.

Often we equate repentance with some kind of emotional experience or an invitation given at the close of a church service to take some specific action. Without question, many have experienced genuine repentance at such times. But it isn't the invitation or the location that is the mark of authentic repentance; it's the attitude of the heart and mind. Whatever my sinful behavior, I acknowledge that I have violated God's standards. I not only admit to what I've done, but by His grace I choose to turn from it to Him. The sinful behavior may be adultery, child abuse, cheating on one's income tax, misusing authority at work, or even hidden sins such as jealous anger or coveting. I say unequivocally that it is wrong, it is counter to God's character, and by His grace I choose to turn from it to the Lord.

What we are talking about is not simply a glib "Forgive me, Lord, for I have sinned." As C. S. Lewis once said,

> The trouble is that what we call "asking God's forgiveness" very often really consists in asking God to accept our excuses. What leads us into this mistake is the fact that there is usually some amount of excuse, some "extenuating circumstances." We are so very apt to point these out to God (and to ourselves) that we forget the really important thing; that is, the bit left over, the bit which the excuses don't cover, the bit which is inexcusable but not, thank God, unforgivable.[1]

It's a clear distinction, yet one we often allow to become muddied. An excuse does not make sin excusable. We must take responsibility, own the sin, and confess our part.

But sin is not unforgivable. For that, we must trust God.

Absolute Trust

Which brings us to the third of our steps for prodigals: absolute trust. This means placing complete trust in Him to direct and empower us to live in a way that pleases Him. No more trying to do it ourselves or figuring out what's right or wrong from our own preferences or desires. No more attempting to turn over a new leaf or trying to pull it off in the power of our human selves. As Paul pointed out in Colossians 2:6–7, the successful Christian life operates on the same faith principle as salvation. Just as we receive the Lord, so we are to live—by faith.

Remember, Jesus never told His disciples, "Without Me you can do very little." His clear-cut statement, as relevant to us as to them, was, ". . . without Me you can do nothing" (John 15:5).

It may seem strange to think of trust in terms of our human conscience. However, the Greek word for "conscience" in the New Testament, *sundesis*, is a compound word meaning "to know with."[2] It describes that internal guide, much like a compass, that God has given to point us in the direction of obedience. The purpose of conscience is to enable us "to discern both good and evil" (Hebrews 5:14). Paul labels the conscience "the work of the Law written in their hearts" that excuses or accuses us with regard to pleasing or displeasing God (Romans 2:15). Just as a hiker walking through deep woods or an aviator flying above the clouds must trust a compass for the proper bearings, the prodigal, especially one who has refused to hear God's Word, must listen to the tug of conscience toward the loving Father.

Our consciences, however, will typically try to mislead us in one of two ways. On the one hand, conscience may attempt to tell us that what we've done isn't so bad. Maybe it's a little white lie, but it's not really a big sin. This kind of message is the product of what Paul referred to as a seared conscience (1 Timothy 4:2). You can understand how this works if you've ever burned your tongue while drinking hot coffee.

Both of us have become known at Back to the Bible for our fondness for coffee. Generally, we like to have a fresh cup in hand when we go into the studio to record a program. But we both have learned the hard way the importance of carefully sipping that hot cup of coffee to avoid scalding the tongue and rendering our taste buds useless for our next meal.

So it is with the conscience. Persistent living in denial, rebellion, and prodigal behavior will sear the conscience so we cannot trust it to tell us when we are violating biblical principles.

Then there is the weak conscience. Paul discussed this concept at length in his New Testament letters, Romans and 1 Corinthians. He pointed out how a weak conscience frequently leads a person to set up arbitrary standards for pleasing God. Weak consciences render us ineffective in practicing Christian love because we will tend to accuse others unfairly when they violate our own false standards (1 Corinthians 8:7).

When we turn from prodigalism, God wants us to develop a clear conscience, one that in maturity and openness to the truth of the Word enables us to live honestly before God and others (Hebrews 13:18). It reflects a life in which God is set apart in our hearts so that our words and behavior exalt Him (1 Peter 3:16).

There is an incredibly important balance involved in our response to God, balance in trusting the Lord who promised to forgive the prodigal behaviors we've confessed and in obeying Him as a way of life.

Uncompromising Obedience

Finally, we need to begin to live in uncompromising obedience to the Lord God. The term for "obedience" used so prominently throughout the New Testament is the Greek word *hupakouo* which is also translated as "submission." It involves two basic elements: the prefix *hupo* carries the idea of submitting while *akouó* means to listen. First of all, we are to pay attention to what God has said and then take what He has said so seriously that we submit to Him as the authority of our lives.

Now we don't need a degree in Greek to grasp what this means. Any parent of a child can understand it.

When the Bible says "Children obey your parents," it means that children are to listen to hear what their parents have to say; then they should submit to what they've been told.

Suppose, for example, you hand your five-year-old daughter a bowl of ice cream and say, "Eat this in the kitchen." The five-year-old looks at you and promptly wanders into the living room, then spills the three colors of cold Neapolitan all over your carpet. She didn't obey which is the same as saying she didn't submit.

Later, your teenage son heads out the door for the evening, your treasured set of car keys in hand. "Be sure to be home by 11:30 or call." At 12:30, he walks through the door, spots the stern look on your face, and says, "I didn't hear you give me a time to be home!" He too failed to obey. Part of the responsibility of obedience is to listen for instructions.

So it is in our relationship with God. And how do we listen for His instructions? Clearly by spending time in His Word. The Bible is the key to a clean life. As the psalmist learned, "Your word is a lamp to my feet and a light to my path" (Psalm 119:105). It is the key to continued, uncompromising obedience. That's why it is so critical for all of us, especially those of us who have just turned from the prodigal path, to have a regular quiet time to carefully read and study God's Word, allowing Him to pinpoint any sin so that we can confess it to Him and allow Him to direct our steps.

Being part of a local church that preaches and teaches the Bible is important so that we can experience spiritual growth and direction for life. The fellowship, accountability, and encouragement from other

Christians is a key part of what it takes to keep us from the deceitful trap of sin (Hebrews 3:13). Regular exposure to the teaching of God's Word, both in the local church and through Christian radio ministries such as Back to the Bible, can also provide us with the kind of spiritual nutrition we need to live in submission to God's Word.

That's what had happened in Ron's life. He faced the failures of his previous lifestyle and honestly confessed the way he had sinned against God. Genuinely repentant, he trusted the Lord to forgive him, then purposed to live a life of uncompromising obedience.

Since then, Ron has had a part in leading his third wife to personal faith in Christ. He, his wife, and the two children God has given them are now active in a local church. Ron is seeking to walk with the Lord and lead others to faith in Him. His is a ministry of reaching out to others who have found themselves on the prodigal path.

"I'm always delighted to help them find the way home," he says with a smile.

Endnotes

1. C. S. Lewis "On Forgiveness," *The Weight of Glory* (New York: MacMillan, 1947), 122–23.

2. W. E. Vine, *An Expository Dictionary of New Testament Words* (Nashville: Thomas Nelson, 1984), 220.

CHAPTER SIXTEEN

Getting the Prodigal's Attention

God whispers to us in our pleasures, speaks in our conscience, but shouts in our pains. It is His megaphone to rouse a deaf world.

—C. S. Lewis

In August, 1969, hurricane Camille threatened the Gulf coast. Radio and television stations broadcast a hurricane watch which was soon upgraded to a hurricane warning. Some paid attention, boarded up their homes, packed up their essential belongings, and left the coastal area for higher ground.

Many others chose not to heed the warnings. Some threw hurricane parties; others simply decided to ride the storm out. "I've been through hurricanes before," one resident told a reporter. "Life goes on."

Tragically, life ended for over two hundred individuals when Camille came crashing ashore. Hurricane parties were turned into death traps in many instances—all because people didn't pay attention to the warnings.

God Knows How

God certainly knows how to get our attention when He wants to speak to us. In the life of Jonah, God used a terrifying storm to get him to see just how serious it was to be headed in the opposite direction from where God wanted him to go. After the prodigal prophet spent three days in the stomach of a massive fish, he finally obeyed God. Miriam suffered the shame and devastation of leprosy because of her rebellion. For David the misery of many sleepless nights came to a climax when he heard those stinging words of rebuke from Nathan, "You are the man!"

Every true believer who has wandered from the way of righteousness and chosen a lifestyle of disobedience and sin will have to contend with the fact that God will pursue. It was the poet Francis Thompson who vividly described God's pursuit of the prodigal as a relentless "hound of heaven."

Sometimes God speaks quietly through His Word. Sometimes He works more firmly through people. Often, He uses events—even tragic ones.

His real name was not Vernon, but we'll call him that. He came to college to prepare for ministry, and the students and faculty he met thought at first his arm was in a sling because he had sprained it. Later, they learned Vern's arm was totally disabled.

After a time, Vern faced a painful decision. He could continue to wear the arm in a sling, hoping he might regain some use; however, the doctors recommended that he have it removed and be fitted with a prosthesis, an artificial arm. After agonizing over the decision, seeking advice from family and friends, pastor, parents, and advisors at school, he made the decision: the arm would be removed.

For Vern, the arm in the sling and the prosthesis provided a vivid reminder of how God had dealt with him about committing his life to Him and serving Him.

Vern had resisted the Lord, his Christian parents, and others. He didn't need anybody telling him what to do. He was perfectly capable of making his own decisions.

During a time when he was running from God, Vern was involved in a serious motorcycle accident. He recovered from the rest of his multiple injuries, but doctors told him he would never regain the use of his arm.

While recovering from the accident, with plenty of time to think, Vern began to open his heart to the Lord. He later admitted, "I paid a terrible price for God to get my attention."

Betty experienced similar circumstances. Early in her high school career, she had been active in her youth group. Then, almost overnight, she turned away from the Lord and her Christian friends to hang out with a crowd of people who were involved in drugs, alcohol, and immoral behavior.

Betty soon became pregnant. Still refusing to listen to God's voice, she chose to have an abortion. Angrily, she told her parents, "It'll never happen again."

But it did. Within a year, Betty had become pregnant for the second time. Finally, loving friends broke through her wall of denial. She poured out her heart to God and confessed her wayward behavior. With her parents' help, she kept the baby, a beautiful young son whom she named Joshua because, as she put it, "I've chosen to serve the Lord now."

Her turn to the Lord didn't prevent the painful consequences of her behavior. Thankfully, as she put it, "I could finally hear God speaking to me. He even used the tragedy of the abortion to get my attention. It was my choice, and it was so wrong. I'm still dealing with the consequences and the pain, but I know now that God has forgiven me, and I'll see my baby in heaven. I've committed myself to the Lord, to live a clean life for Him from here on."

In Betty's case there were individuals who cared enough to confront her with the wrongness of her behavior. "They told me the truth, but they did so in love," she recalled. "I didn't want to listen to them. I didn't think they cared about me, and I didn't care to hear what they had to say. I'm glad now they cared enough to keep after me."

Pattern for Loving Confrontation

In his instructional letter to a new group of Christians, the apostle Paul provided a framework for relating to people, including those who are prodigals. He encouraged them with the truth about their future in the presence of the Lord Jesus—caught up to meet the Lord in the air, they would be reunited with fellow Christians who had already died. The apostle urged them to encourage and build each other up in the faith, just as they were already doing (1 Thessalonians 5:11). Then, after instructing them on how to show respect for their pastoral leaders (vv. 12–13), he encouraged them regarding three categories of struggling believers.

First, he told them to confront those who are out of line. The word he used for "unruly," *ataktous*, was a military term which carried the idea of a person being out of step. Some people are actively out of line, choosing to head off into sinful behaviors as Betty did. Others, including some in the early church, had become passively out of line, choosing to shun their personal responsibilities (2 Thessalonians 3:11). Paul's point was that those who were out of line needed to have their thinking challenged and to be confronted with the truth of God's Word.

Such confrontation was always to be done in love (Ephesians 4:15). It's too bad that many of us equate love with softness and an unwillingness to challenge wrong thinking or behaviors. To use the term in common use today, biblical love is always "tough love." It doesn't continually harangue the prodigal, but it refuses to simply ignore or look the other way when someone is headed in the wrong direction. It is likely that the father of the prodigal confronted his wayward son on several occasions before he left.

The second word of instruction Paul gave was to cheer up those who were at the point of quitting. The term Paul used to describe these individuals literally means "short souled"—it indicates that a crisis has occurred. When Betty discovered she was pregnant the second time, both she and her parents faced such a crisis. As she was confronted with her sinful behavior, she confessed it and turned to the Lord and His people. Her parents also owned the failures they saw in their lives. To continue to confront or condemn Betty and her parents for failing would have been unchristian. The appropriate thing to do at this point was to provide encouragement and help. That's precisely what the church family stepped in and did.

Some Christians have the idea that confrontation is the only appropriate tool to use. Paul confirms that there is a time to confront, but by implication he suggests there is a time not to confront. The prodigal's father clearly modeled this when he refused to play the "I told you so" game or to berate the prodigal son when he returned.

A third strategy recommended by the apostle is to support those with long-term weaknesses. The term can refer to a physical, an emotional, or a moral and spiritual weakness. In the case of Betty, there had clearly been some long-term weaknesses that had led to her past failures. Insightfully, Betty's pastor asked one of the mature younger women in the church to work with her in an accountability relationship. He also recommended she see a Christian counselor he knew. Also, she developed a new set of friends who didn't have the same immoral values and behaviors as her former friends.

As we have seen, Betty benefited from all three strategies recommended by the apostle Paul: confrontation when she was out of line, encouragement and help when she reached a point of crisis and could have given up, and ongoing support to deal with her long-term weaknesses.

There are two implications to what we have considered in this chapter. First, when God wants to get our attention, we'd best pay heed. If what's going on in our lives—whether the rebuke of a friend, the gnawing ache of a guilty conscience, or the pressure of consequences—hasn't gotten through to us, God knows precisely and lovingly just how much to turn up the heat so we will respond.

Second, it is imperative that we be willing to take on that loving role and provide whatever the prodigal individuals in our lives need: loving confrontation for wayward behavior, helpful concern when they feel overwhelmed and are ready to quit, or long-term support to help them deal with the weaknesses that may be left over from their prodigal behavior pattern.

Helping a Prodigal

It's so important we recognize that while prodigals have strayed from God's path, they've never wandered from His heart. Perhaps that prodigal in your life has strayed from your presence. It's important to make sure he or she hasn't wandered away from your heart. And how do you achieve that?

First, love your prodigal. This requires that the communication lines remain open. Whenever you have contact with him or her, show genuine care, compassion, and concern. Encourage the prodigal in whatever way you can. Make clear that even though you may reject some of the behaviors, you don't reject him or her as a person.

Second, pray for prodigals. Pray every day, expecting God to answer your prayers. Remember that Jesus emphasized in His teaching on prayer that we are to always pray and never give up (Luke 18:1). Ask God to convict them of sin and to bring them to repentance. Ask Him to bring people and circumstances into their lives that will touch them.

Third, be patient. It's so easy to "write off" a prodigal, to conclude that he or she is a "lost cause." The example of the prodigal's father should stand as a monumental warning against ever giving up on someone. Jesus didn't say how long the son had been gone, but the story seems to indicate a minimum of months if not years.

Fourth, avoid harboring pent-up resentment or bitterness toward your prodigal. Remember how the father in Jesus' parable refused to become bitter. This is an important consideration, both while the prodigal is away and when he or she returns. Remember Paul's warning to put away all bitterness and to respond with kindness, tenderheartedness, and forgiveness (Ephesians 4:30–32).

Finally, whenever a tough love approach becomes necessary within a family or when discipline is undertaken by a local church, always act in a spirit of truth and love. Make sure the facts are in order and everything is done according to truth. And be sure to encourage the person while dealing firmly with sinful behaviors.

As Betty reflected over her prodigal behavior, her eyes filled with tears. She sat in her parents' living room holding her baby, and a smile crossed her face.

"I really thought God was being so unfair to let me get pregnant. Then I even blamed Him for the abortion—and I was so bitter toward the baby's father.

"But now I know God just wanted to get my attention. I'm glad He used my sister, Linda, and my parents. Plus my pastor, my youth pastor, and others."

God will use circumstances and people to get a prodigal's attention just like He did with Betty. He does so because He cares about each one and because He wants each to turn from the prodigal way back to Him.

CHAPTER SEVENTEEN

How to Prevent Prodigal Fallout

We believe that the power behind us is greater than the task ahead.

—Motto of a local church

"For about ten years, my life was like a yo-yo," Johnny explained as he sat in an easy chair in his den. "I just went back and forth on a beaten path. Running from God, caught up in the pleasures of sin. Then back to church, usually during the spring or fall revival services we had. Down the aisle, tearful repentance, living for the Lord for a while. Then back into the old rut."

Sound familiar? Unfortunately, that's the well-worn path of many prodigals—like spiritual bungee jumpers who keep leaping off the deep end, seeing how close they can come to total disaster, always confident they can somehow bounce back. Yet they never quite seem to bounce back to the heights where they once were.

We're convinced there's an antidote to what we call "prodigal fallout," that all-too-common tendency of those who have returned home to turn again to prodigalism—either of the same kind or some other wayward behavior of a different form.

It seems the old, common sense adage of Ben Franklin's that an ounce of prevention is worth a pound of cure has a great deal of practical significance for prodigals.

After we have honestly confessed our prodigal behavior to God, have genuinely repented, have turned to Him in absolute trust, and have begun walking in uncompromising obedience, how can we keep from slipping and falling into the same trap?

Recognize God's Work

We begin by recognizing the validity and power of the process by which God brought us back. God has indeed done a work in our lives and for this we need to be incredibly grateful. Failing to properly give thanks to God for all His benefits, especially when He has drawn us back to Himself, places us at greater risk for future failure (see Psalm 103:2).

Perhaps that's what happened to the prodigal church in Ephesus. "Prodigal church?" you say. That's exactly right. This church had experienced the blessing of the apostle Paul's teaching and the leadership of Paul's protégé, Timothy. They had learned the deep things of God.

When John wrote to the pastor of this church near the end of the first century, he acknowledged their hard labor, patience, doctrinal purity, and intense service without giving up (Revelation 2:1–3). Yet he also pinpointed a very important weakness. These believers had left their first love (v. 4). He didn't say their first love had left them—they had left their first love.

We are convinced that the seeds of prodigal behavior often take root and begin to flourish when the fervor of our love for the Lord begins to wane. It's the kind of thing that often happens in a marriage. Two people fall in love and marry. During the early years there is an intensity in their love for each other.

Then things begin to slip. They take each other for granted and gradually stop communicating with each other. He becomes wrapped up in work and she with the children. It's not that they've fallen out of love, it's just they've left the priority of that love relationship. That's how it frequently happens between us and the Lord.

One of the most important ways to keep the fervency of our love for the Lord kindled is to spend time with Him. For both of us, reading the Bible early in the morning has become a key to preventing prodigal behavior. So make sure that you guard your priority of reading the Bible and cultivating the personal warmth of your relationship with Him. Be aware of His presence in your activities throughout the day. Like Moses, endure "as seeing Him who is invisible" (Hebrews 11:27). Make sure you talk with Him during the day, following Paul's instructions to "pray without ceasing" (1 Thessalonians 5:17).

Also, make sure you have really returned to the place from where you strayed. There may have been fences that were trampled when you ran away from the Lord or barriers erected between you and someone else by your sinful behavior. Make sure the fences have been mended and any barriers you built have been broken down. It is appropriate to ask forgiveness of heartbroken parents, of alienated brothers and sisters, and of offended church family and friends. Sure, some may act like the older brother, but choose to forgive them anyway. Remember the incredible forgiveness which God has lovingly extended to you. Be sure to tell those who loved you and prayed for you while you were away how much you appreciate their concern and forgiveness.

Then, make the spiritual disciplines of godly living a priority. Time in the Bible daily, asking the Spirit to open your eyes to its truths and honestly seeking to apply them, is a must. Regular time in meaningful prayer, voicing your needs to God and lifting up others to Him is another key priority. So is fellowship with other believers and the regular teaching of God's Word that you can find in a Bible-believing local church.

Look as well for ways to serve God. It may be that some areas of service are not open to you because of your past prodigal behavior. On the other hand, whole new vistas for ministry may now be a part of your life.

That's what happened to Harold, who had spent time as the

successful pastor of a small church following his graduation from seminary. However, Harold's hard-driving, type-A personality had caused him to neglect his wife and children. Before long, his marriage dissolved.

When Harold admitted to his own failure in his marriage and sought help, God opened up a side of his life he had previously been unaware of. He became involved in an administrative capacity at a Christian camp and discovered he had both administrative and counseling skills which he could effectively use for the Lord.

In addition, be aware of your particular weakness. While the potential is present for any of us to be tempted in any area, it's likely that each of us has a bent to a sin, a particular area of temptation which easily ensnares us. Perhaps it is the sin of drunkenness, complicated by a long-running addiction to alcohol. It may be a weakness toward sexual immorality, fostered by a tendency to give in to the lure of pornographic literature. Or it may be a weakness toward pride, complicated by a Pharisaic "elder brother" attitude toward those who succumb to sexual and materialistic temptations. Whatever our weaknesses are, we need to be aware of them and remain on the alert. As Paul so wisely warned the Corinthians, "Therefore let him who thinks he stands take heed lest he fall" (1 Corinthians 10:12).

Furthermore, ask for prayer and encouraging support from God's people to help you keep from wandering away from Him the way you did in the first place. However, Satan will see to it that the path of prodigalism is smooth and easy, filled with tempting allures. Remember the exhortation of Ecclesiastes 4:12, "Though one may be overpowered by another, two can withstand him. And a threefold cord is not quickly broken."

Finally, open yourself up to becoming accountable to a supportive group of individuals. For a man, this may mean two or three spiritually mature men; for a woman, perhaps a like number of older women. Generally we find it most helpful to have two or three people close to your age and background level, plus one or two older, more mature individuals who can serve as mentors.

Accountability means you allow them the opportunity to ask you the tough questions, and you promise to be honest in responding to them about your walk with the Lord, the kind of temptation you are facing, and the way you are handling it.

Following these steps doesn't guarantee you will never struggle again or that you will not fall. However, they can help keep you from returning to the prodigal path.

CHAPTER EIGHTEEN

Avoid Being an Older Brother

O would some Power the gift give us
To see ourselves as others see us!

—Robert Burns

"I just can't understand it!" Chuck exclaimed as he slammed his hand down on the table. The rest of the men in the room looked at him with a mixture of surprise, indignation, and sadness. "There's just not enough commitment these days. Too many people dropping out of church!

"I'm really exasperated about Andy. I spent so much time with him, tried to disciple him. Now look! Just because his wife has left him, he decides to up and drop out of church, stays away for months, then has the audacity to come back and think we'll take him right back in.

"I just think we're too soft on sin these days. It's time we sent a message to those people who may be considering dropping out. We need to make it tougher for those kind of people to get back into church."

Prodigals can be found both in families and in churches. And wherever you find prodigals, you're likely to discover older brothers. As we mentioned earlier, an older brother is simply a prodigal of a different kind. None of the other elders who attended the board meeting where Chuck pounded the table and voiced his opinion about taking prodigals back in would have considered Chuck a prodigal. After all, he and his family were always the first ones at church every Sunday morning—a fact they prided themselves on. They were also the last ones to leave after services. Chuck made no bones about the importance of being at church "every time the doors are open," and he was faithful not only in tithing but in giving above and beyond his regular share to missions and other projects.

But Chuck was a prodigal all right, even though his fellow church members would never have thought of him that way. His was the pharisaic "older brother" prodigalism we described at length back in chapter 6—the kind that from all external appearances seems to never have wandered away from the father but in matters of the heart is as far away as the prodigal in a distant land. We are convinced that the older brother kind of prodigals can cause just as much grief to the church family as those who have wandered off into sin.

Andy was typical of many "younger brother" prodigals today. Because of several factors, including his own slipping spiritual life, conflicts with other church members, and a growing indifference, he no longer considered it helpful or comfortable to continue as an active part of his church family. Andy didn't formally sever his relationship with the church. Instead, like the prodigal son in Scripture, he simply decided that he no longer needed his church family. He could make it on his own.

Sometimes modern-day prodigals like Andy become so disillusioned with the church that they formally break off relationship with the local congregation, vowing never to return. More commonly, such individuals simply stop attending church, often waiting to see if anyone notices that they are missing. They simply move on when they perceive that no one seems to care.[1]

When a modern prodigal leaves a local church, you might say he takes his inheritance along with him—the wealth of love, care, training, and fellowship he has received from being a part of his church family. He leaves a supportive fellowship for a world void of the spiritual resources which could encourage him to return in loving obedience to the Lord.

Even more sad is the fact that when he leaves the church, he has turned his back on his loving heavenly Father. Rejecting the God to whom he owes everything, the modern prodigal makes his way to a spiritually-distant realm where he tries to fill his hunger with spiritual carob pods and worldly husks.

Back at the Church

Meanwhile, back at the church, continuing to occupy his pew and fulfill his responsibilities, is that other kind, the older brother prodigal. Now this prodigal would *never* entertain the notion that he should ever wear such a label. If you asked him, he would quickly let you know he would never follow the example of the prodigal son. With the intensity of Peter's fervent assertion, "I'd never deny You, Lord," this individual would tell you in no uncertain terms that he would never leave the church, never quit fellowshipping with God's people. That just wouldn't be his style!

Yet in several respects, such individuals show a remarkable similarity to the prodigal son's older brother.

First, the modern older brother is usually the epitome of faithful service. Whenever the church is open, he is right there in his place, dressed appropriately, Bible in hand, perhaps even with a pad for taking notes. He always says the right things, does the right things—in fact, he is as well-acquainted with all the biblical terminology and spiritual jargon as anyone else. His faithfulness may include tithing, serving on the church board, perhaps teaching a Sunday school class, or participating in a group Bible study. People usually look up to such an individual.

Such a person typically has a good job and a nice comfortable home, the results of his admirable self-discipline and work ethic. People are frequently impressed with his family. His kids usually conform to Christian standards—at least outwardly. This individual is an upstanding member of the community. He contributes to community projects, tries to obey the traffic laws, and generally does what is right.

Performance Trap

But there is one fatal flaw in his pattern of behavior. This older brother kind of prodigal (a man or a woman) tries to serve the church and the heavenly Father out of duty rather than love. The financial contribution he makes to his church comes from his billfold or his checking account but not from his heart. He is willing to donate hours of manual labor—in fact he may be incensed that others are unwilling to work—but his primary motivation involves winning his heavenly Father's approval while making sure others are aware of his superior level of commitment. She is often more concerned about making sure that the Sunday school rooms are spotlessly clean and in order than that the children who use them learn spiritual truth. He cares more about the undusted bookracks that hold the hymnals on the pew backs or the correct and customary order of service than he is about seeing the spiritual needs of hurting people being met in the service.

He or she is a modern-day carbon copy of the prodigal son's older brother, a man who served his father and his community faithfully—at least according to outward appearances. That brother kept the letter of the law but not its spirit. He served his father out of a sense of responsibility, even though it didn't seem all that rewarding. The essence of his relationship with his father was bondage not love. And his feeling toward his absent brother was even worse. The impression Jesus gave in telling the story was that the elder brother could care less if his younger brother ever returned. There was no concern over where he was or what he was doing. Perhaps he felt that if his prodigal brother came home, it would just disrupt things for him.

Today's twentieth-century older brother has much the same attitude. She hasn't prayed for the prodigals who have left the church family. Nor has he bothered to look for a way to draw them back. She can give you an earful about the single mother who stopped coming to church, but she never took the time to look beyond her behavior to see how she and others never made her feel welcome. He was quick with a sarcastic remark about the young couple who attended for a few Sundays then were seen no more, but he never lifted their names to the heavenly Father in prayer. No, he just wrote them all off.

Now he may on occasion shake hands with a visitor and hand him or her a bulletin or a visitor's card, but his welcome never goes beyond the surface. In fact, there are times when she winces when someone who is inappropriately dressed walks into church. It annoys him that some of the college group look a bit too scruffy for his liking. And while she can express her desire for the church to grow, deep inside she's pretty comfortable with the people, size, and church situation she's come to be familiar with.

Henry and Suzy were typical modern-day older brothers. When they got wind that Cheryl had filed a legal separation against her husband, a graduate of a Christian college and a fairly faithful member in their church, they immediately went to see the pastor and voice their righteous indignation against her being allowed to continue to sing in the choir. After all, the church's reputation was at stake. They'd feel a lot more comfortable if the church board would just take disciplinary action and kick her out.

Their lack of compassion was only exceeded by their lack of knowledge of Cheryl's real circumstances. What they didn't realize was that Cheryl had been the victim of domestic violence for more than a year. In fact, the previous Sunday she had sung in the choir only after using heavy makeup to cover a black eye her husband had given her the night before. Her husband was one of those individuals who appeared to be as upright as anyone else, but who secretly was addicted to episodes of rage.

In similar fashion, many other modern-day older brothers demonstrate a lack of compassion for those in pain or in need. They may think the homeless ought to just find a place to live or that anyone who happens to be unemployed is probably lazy and could get a job if he or she just wanted to. They have little sympathy for or desire to help drug abusers or alcoholics. In short, these individuals are modern-day, self-righteous, church-going Pharisees. The only things missing are the long robes and the phylacteries—the ceremonial pouches worn on arm and forehead by the Pharisees of Jesus' day who wanted to appear to be devout (Matthew 23:5).

Condemning Sin

Such individuals are usually quite skilled at identifying and condemning sin in the lives of others. They feel justified in looking askance at individuals who don't "fit in" with those who know all the spiritual code words. They feel more comfortable with people who pretend to have no needs or weaknesses than with those who are open about them. They have little or no concern about anyone who doesn't meet their criteria of "spiritual correctness."

How do such individuals react when a prodigal returns to the church family and is welcomed with open arms? Typically, you don't find any tears of joy in the older brother's eyes. No praise for the wanderers return in his heart. No, the older brother usually feels ignored and alone, jealous and unappreciated.

"What's the deal here? I've been faithful in the church all along. I've done everything I was called on to do, but no one seems to notice. Nobody cares!

"Why, they just open their arms to any and every sinner. It's a disgrace! What will the citizens of our community think if we let these people back in? The next thing you know, they'll ask them to be ushers or teach a Bible study class—maybe even my class!"

Even though Chuck picked up some sympathetic expressions of agreement from others on the board and in the church, he was wrong and out of line. In fact, his pastor needed to love him enough to graciously confront him—and he did.

By doing so, Chuck's pastor followed the example of a first-century apostle who confronted a similar "older brother." The apostle's name was John, and the older brother was Diotrephes.

Near the end of his life, John wrote three brief letters which are included in the New Testament. What we now know as 3 John was addressed to a close friend named Gaius. The church in which Gaius was involved had been practicing Christian hospitality, and John was delighted to commend them for this and other evidences that they were walking in the truth.

Then John turned his attention to Diotrephes. According to the apostle, this man had engaged in malicious gossip, rejecting John's apostolic authority and refusing to receive those who came to the church. In fact, Diotrephes misused church discipline by kicking individuals out of the church inappropriately and with a vindictive motive (3 John 10).

The attitudes of twentieth-century Chuck and first-century Diotrephes are remarkably similar since the underlying problem with each was a buildup of long-term bitterness and resentment. According to the author of Hebrews, such an attitude is extremely dangerous because it can lead to spiritual pollution and destruction (Hebrews 12:15).

Another wrong motivation, shared by Diotrephes and Chuck and commonly found in older brothers, is pride. When John noted that Diotrephes was fond of the preeminence (3 John 9), he employed a word found only one other time in the entire New Testament. That singular usage, however, speaks volumes because it is used to describe Christ who is to have preeminence in all things (Colossians 1:18). To love preeminence is to usurp that which belongs to Jesus alone. It constitutes pride which is first on the list of those sins hated by the Lord (Proverbs 6:17). It's a lethal combination: pride and bitterness.

Individuals like Chuck and Diotrephes may think they are defending the reputation and life of the church. Yet pride has blinded them to their own sinful motives, while bitterness has short-circuited any possibility of authentic compassion.

Facing the Truth

One of the hardest things for any Christian to do is face the truth when he or she has responded like an older brother. For some reason, it's often far easier to admit to being a prodigal.

So how should you respond if you look into the mirror of God's Word and discover some older brother tendencies?

The right approach is to do exactly what the prodigal son did! First, face the truth. Honestly confess your sin. Come to yourself and recognize that your attitudes and behavior have actually been prodigal in nature. In essence, what we're talking about is repentance—repentance of the sins of jealously, anger, bitterness, resentment, pride, a lack of love, and anything else the Lord may convict you of.

When you've done this, you are ready to be reconciled to your heavenly Father. Plus, you can enjoy fellowship with those prodigals who have also returned to Him and to the community of faith.

One final thought: go back and review the suggestions on how to help the prodigal. Look for opportunities to put them into action. Then determine by God's grace to remain spiritually sensitive and compassionate, so you can avoid falling into the trap of being an older brother again.

Endnotes

1. For an excellent book on the topic of church dropouts, see *Exit Interviews* by William Hendricks (Chicago: Moody Press, 1993).

CHAPTER NINETEEN

Those Who Love Prodigals

Success is failure turned inside out,
The silver tint of the clouds of doubt,
And you never can tell just how close you are,
It may be near when it seems so far
So stick to the fight when you're hardest hit —
You must not quit.

— Anonymous

Perhaps you have felt the vibration and sudden draft caused by a door being slammed in your face by a prodigal son or daughter. Your heart has been pierced with the pain of an angry vow never to return. That's what the parents of Lynne heard one evening just after midnight, when they confronted their daughter over her return home more than an hour past her curfew.

"I've had it with both of you and with this home! I don't intend to ever live here again! I don't know where I'm going, but I'm not staying here!" Then the door slammed, and there was only an angry silence.

Perhaps your prodigal still lives in your home, unreasonable and arrogant, shutting you out of his life. Every day your stomach churns and your heart aches as you see him squandering hours and days in the futile pursuits that Solomon called "chasing after the wind."

That's what the parents of Eddie went through. "It wasn't so much the hair down to his shoulders, the earring, or the strange clothes," Eddie's father told a friend. "It wasn't even the night we almost came to blows over my telling him where he could and couldn't go. It was just his constant attitude of 'you're not telling me what to do no matter what.' "

Or your prodigal may be a spouse who has wandered away from the relationship, become attracted to someone else, or perhaps even pursued an affair. This too will create devastating pain, incredible self-doubt, and intense anger.

Yet the story Jesus told about the prodigal son provides hope for every prodigal situation, mainly because of the picture of a human father who reflects our compassionate heavenly Father.

This father always held on to the hope of his prodigal's return. He didn't attempt to block his younger son's excursion into his wayward path. Nor did he fall into the trap some modern parents slip into who think that teenage misconduct can be eliminated by simply controlling outward behavior. This father didn't bother telling his son how unwise he was. He didn't refuse to grant the portion of his inheritance or try to take other extraordinary measures to prevent this foolishness.

The father didn't pursue his son through the pigpen. He could have—and some modern parents do—but he chose not to. He didn't organize a search party, hire a detective agency, or begin calling anyone and everyone he suspected might know where his son was.

Charlene, distraught and upset, told her pastor, "This is the fifth time our son has run away. We've just about exhausted our money, and his father and I are at our wits end. What can we do?" When Charlene's pastor suggested they not pursue their eighteen-year-old son, the mother expressed shock. "How could we not pursue him? After all, we love him."

With insight and compassion, Charlene's pastor explained that genuine love is not simply an emotion, but an act of the will. It doesn't always pursue but looks to do what is best. Authentic love doesn't always seek to meet one's own need for love and acceptance, which is frequently the motivation behind parents who keep pursuing their older runaways. Rather, true love always seeks God's best for the one loved.

Apparently the prodigal's father had learned that lesson. He didn't chase his son, but he never gave up hope of his return. Every day he looked for him. He must have tucked away those special gifts for when he returned—a beautiful ring and a majestic robe. He kept a calf in the feed lot, well fattened.

In the same way, God has prepared a delightful welcome for prodigals who return to Him. And when the prodigal son finally responded to the painful consequences that motivated him to turn back toward home, his father greeted him with love and affection, forgiveness and joy. So, too, the heavenly Father waits to forgive and restore His lost sheep and reconcile them to Himself.

Perhaps you are wondering in your own mind about the wisdom of the response by the prodigal's father. Why not go after the prodigal, restrain him forcibly if necessary, and drag him back kicking and screaming? After all, then he would be rescued from harming himself further and from doing more damage to the name of the Lord.

The answer is as old as the reason why God gave our original parents the option of choosing to do right or wrong. God wants willing obedience, and unless the response is willing, there has been no real change of heart, only an outward conformity. When delinquents are forced to conform, we fall back into pharisaism. Furthermore, the person who is forced to do right will simply become delinquent again, whenever he or she has the opportunity.

It must have been extremely painful for this father to allow his son the freedom to fail, but he did.

A recap of some of the prodigals whose actions have filled the pages of Scripture reinforces the lesson: God lovingly used circumstances, including times of great difficulty and disaster, to prompt a loving response. He never forces a robot-like conformity to His will.

Nathan and David

In a sense, Nathan was like the father of a prodigal son. Perhaps it would be more accurate to describe him as the friend of a prodigal king. Scripture doesn't give us any record of his thoughts or actions before his confrontation with David, but it isn't hard to imagine this godly man spending hours in prayer, seeking direction for what would surely be the confrontation of his life. Without question, he was taking his life into his hands by confronting David in this way. Any man who demonstrated such a callous disregard for human life by having one of his closest military associates put to death could just have easily snapped his fingers and pointed to Nathan, and the prophet would have been history!

How Nathan's heart must have ached for the king to whom God had given so much, for the ruler who had set such a poor example as a husband and father and had committed adultery and murder. Perhaps he wept for the man who had once loved God so deeply and who had written so many great songs of worship and praise.

Finally, under the prodding and power of the Spirit, Nathan confronted David, and God moved David's heart. David was gripped with conviction, and he repented in sorrow. Nathan's prayers were answered.

Peter and Steve

Who bore the burden of Peter's prodigal denial? Not his fellow disciples. They were already running for their lives. Not the women who knew him. Their eyes were soon to be filled with tears as they watched the crucifixion of Jesus take place.

Only the Savior, who gave Peter that incredible look of loving concern that prompted him to collapse in bitter tears, carried the pain of this disciple's denial.

Peter had been high on Satan's list of targets. As the Lord had warned, Satan wanted to sift him like wheat. Yet what an encouraging word he had been given—"Peter, I have prayed for you that your faith not fail."

Wouldn't you like to have been present when the Lord appeared to Peter after the Resurrection? We have no record of the conversation, but it must have been something special. We do know Peter continued to be Peter. He insisted on knowing the Lord's plans for John and was corrected for putting his nose where it didn't belong. Later he struggled over the approval of others, waffled on the issue of fellowship with Gentile believers, and was rebuked by the apostle Paul for his duplicity.

Yet the Lord's face must have been beaming in heaven on that incredible day of Pentecost when Peter so boldly proclaimed, "This

Jesus whom you crucified, is both Lord and Christ!" How delighted the Savior must have been with Peter's final written words, ". . . but grow in the grace and knowledge of our Lord and Savior Jesus Christ. To Him be the glory both now and forever" (2 Peter 3:18).

So it is with modern-day prodigals. We heard one telling his story on radio just the other day. His name is Steve Green, and he was being asked by an interviewer about the incredible success of his music ministry.

Without hesitation, Steve explained that his ministry of music developed in the aftermath of a ten-year prodigal period in his life. During that time, a compassionate brother played a key role in drawing him back to the Lord. Out of that experience Steve Green wrote music that has touched the hearts of Christians around the world—songs such as "Broken and Spilled Out" and "People Need the Lord."

The Hardest Part

For those who are the loving brothers, sisters, mothers, fathers, and friends of prodigals, what is the most difficult part? Without question, the waiting. Today we despise waiting. We live in a fast-paced society. We become irritated with the music while holding for a phone call. We race our motors while waiting for the light to turn green. We urge our children, "Hurry up now, don't keep Grandma waiting."

Waiting is something we all do in a variety of settings every day, whether waiting for a traffic jam to clear or for the people in front of us to get through the checkout line at the supermarket.

Most of us, however, would rather not have to wait, yet it is one of the greatest lessons we can learn in life. It is an integral component of hope.[1] In the Old Testament, a family of words describe the simple yet profound concept of waiting.

To wait on God with hope is a stretching experience. In fact, the rich vocabulary used to describe waiting in the Old Testament includes words whose meaning suggests a woven line, a cord, or a piece of cloth. One such term was used of the scarlet cord that Rahab, the prostitute of Jericho, stretched from her window as evidence that she was waiting in hope, trusting in Israel's God.

The prophet Isaiah uses a form of this same word to suggest the ultimate source of renewed strength for those who find they have come to the end of their rope. He explains, "But those who *wait* on the Lord shall renew their strength; they shall mount up with wings like eagles, they shall run and not be weary, they shall walk and not faint" (Isaiah 40:31).

Waiting can be physically exhausting, emotionally draining, and spiritually dehydrating. But God always has a perfect timetable. It's futile for us to suppose we can either slow it down or speed it up.

So the ultimate answer for those of us who care about prodigals today, just as it was for the father of the prodigal in Jesus' parable, is to wait on the Lord. There may be things we can do—like Nathan's loving confrontation of David or Jesus' intercessory prayer for Peter— but the ultimate answer is to wait on the Lord, put our confidence in His perfect timing, and commit ourselves and our prodigals to His purpose and His sovereign care.

He will always do what is best.

A Final Prayer

Father, we pray for the prodigals. We pray that You will keep them safe and that in Your grace You will not permit them to drift into a deeper life of sin. Bind the evil one in their lives. Bring them to their senses, Father, and bring them home.

We pray also for the parents and for each loved one. May the love and comfort that only the Lord Jesus can give be theirs. Hold them in Your loving arms, Father, and encourage them when the days are long and the nights are tearful. Show them Your love, we pray, in the name of the Savior. Amen.

Endnotes

1. For a full discussion of hope and waiting, see *Never Give Up: The Incredible Payoff of Perseverance* by Don Hawkins (Lincoln, NE: Back to the Bible).